"If your church closed today, would anyone care? Would the community even notice? My friend Chris Sonksen's latest book, *Indispensable Church*, helps you answer these questions and gives you a practical guide to impact your community like never before. Its simple approach will equip your church to flood the community with acts of kindness and love. I highly recommend you get it into the hands of everyone you know."

Mark Cole, president and CEO, John Maxwell Co.

"Chris Sonksen has been deep into the health and growth of American churches for years. His voice has greatly helped many pastors and their churches thrive and become more effective and impactful in the heart of their communities. His latest book, *Indispensable Church*, captures the heart of Jesus by inspiring us to take our faith outside the church walls and become the hands and feet of Jesus. It is challenging and practical to every believer who wants to let their light shine."

Scott Wilson, global pastor, The Oaks Church

"Chris Sonksen's new book, *Indispensable Church*, is both candid and compelling. Filled with fresh concepts, this book will reset your priorities and inspire you to greater service. In fact, you'll never see your church and the needs of your community the same way again."

Hal Donaldson, president, Convoy of Hope

"In such divisive times in our nation, this message of love, kindness, and service has never been more prevalent than now. Chris Sonksen has an amazing gift to encourage and unify those from all walks of life to truly start a movement in our communities. This book will bring inspiration, hope, and the belief that we truly can make a difference, appreciate each other, and 'love thy neighbor.'"

Ryan Chiaverini, host, ABC 7's *Windy City LIVE*

"*Indispensable Church* answers the question being asked by many: Is the church essential? Chris Sonksen responds with a definite yes by vividly reminding us that the church isn't a performance on the platform, nor is it people sitting in pews. The church must be more than people passively watching; it must be people actively serving and engaging within their community. The power of this institution God created lies in what it does, not in what it says. Its action gives life to God's Word. Chris points out a crucial truth: before the church can be heard, it must be seen. To which I say, Amen."

Gerald Brooks, DD, DCL, lead pastor,
Grace Church, Plano, Texas

"*Indispensable Church* is a book that is right on time. Never has the American church faced such a combination of challenges ranging from shifting cultural landscapes to changing opinions and attitudes about religion, institutions, and authority structures. Helping the church shine as the hope of the world is not only necessary but critical, and that is what this book is designed to do. It's strategically written to be a resource that helps guide the church into the future as the agent of change God meant for it to be. You will enjoy the encouragement and the challenge found in these pages."

Dr. Clayton King, teaching pastor, NewSpring Church;
founder, Crossroads Summer Camps and Crossroads
Conferences; author of *Reborn* and *Stronger*

"In a world that is more isolated and divided than ever, pastors and leaders everywhere are struggling to meet the growing needs of their community. In *Indispensable Church*, Chris Sonksen has delivered powerful yet practical insights that will help equip and empower the church to rise up and learn the language of love. If you're ready to take the church outside its four walls, then *Indispensable Church* is the book for you."

Jared Ming, lead pastor, Higher Vision Church

indispensable
church

indispensable church

powerful ways to flood your community with love

chris sonksen

BakerBooks

a division of Baker Publishing Group
Grand Rapids, Michigan

Published by Baker Books
a division of Baker Publishing Group
PO Box 6287, Grand Rapids, MI 49516-6287
www.bakerbooks.com

Printed in the United States of America

Library of Congress Cataloging-in-Publication Data
Names: Sonksen, Chris, 1968– author.
Title: Indispensable church : powerful ways to flood your community with love / Chris Sonksen.
Description: Grand Rapids, Michigan : Baker Books, a division of Baker Publishing Group, [2021] | Includes bibliographical references.
Identifiers: LCCN 2020035462 | ISBN 9781540900180 (paperback) | ISBN 9781540901484 (casebound)
Subjects: LCSH: Communities—Religious aspects—Christianity. | Love—Religious aspects—Christianity. | Evangelistic work. | Church work. | Missions.
Classification: LCC BV625 .S585 2021 | DDC 261/.1—dc23
LC record available at https://lccn.loc.gov/2020035462

Scripture quotations are from the *Holy Bible*, New Living Translation, copyright © 1996, 2004, 2007, 2013, 2015 by Tyndale House Foundation. Used by permission of Tyndale House Publishers, Inc., Carol Stream, Illinois 60188. All rights reserved.

Some names and details have been changed to protect the privacy of the individuals involved.

21 22 23 24 25 26 27   7 6 5 4 3 2 1

This book is dedicated to Mila Brave Madrigal. You are our first and at this point our only grandchild. May you live a life fully surrendered to Jesus and fulfill all the potential He has placed inside you. I have prayed it a thousand times and now I pray again: may you be a world changer and difference maker. Know that we love you with all our hearts, and we are cheering you on each day as you run the race set before you.

contents

acknowledgments

Many people have shaped my views, filled my heart, and challenged me to take bold action to advance God's kingdom. This book wouldn't have been possible without them.

Karrie Stewart—You are the true author of this book. You led the way in loving where you live, and because of you, churches across this nation are impacting their communities. Thank you for your compassionate heart to serve and your courageous spirit to lead. We're all better because of you.

Church BOOM Lead Team—You guys are the absolute best. You have such incredible hearts for the local church. You're more concerned with building God's kingdom than expanding your own kingdom. You love pastors, you love leaders, and you love seeing others win. I'm eternally grateful for each of you.

South Hills Church—Every pastor, leader, board member, volunteer, and attender. I love each of you very much, and I'm honored to be a part of your lives. Let's keep making a difference for Jesus.

Hal Donaldson—Over the past several years, I've had the privilege of having a front-row seat to your leadership, and

I've learned so much. You lead with great integrity, a heart filled with compassion, and an abundance of generosity. We've walked through some great times together and have shouldered some difficult ones as well, and in each circumstance, you have been such an incredible friend. I'm so thankful that God brought our paths together. You make me a better person and a better leader.

Pat Springle—You are one of the most talented people I know. Your writing, insights, and understanding make projects like this possible. Thanks for being such an amazing partner.

The team at Baker Publishing Group—Thank you for everything you do: editing, collaborating, creating, suggesting, marketing, and working tirelessly to assure a quality product. Thanks for believing in me and the message of this book.

My agent, Tawny Johnson—You're literally one of my favorite people to talk to. You make work fun and always keep me laughing. I'm sincerely grateful to partner with you, and I look forward to even greater things ahead. Thanks for being the best!

My family—My wife, Laura; my son, Aidan; my daughter, Grace; and my son-in-law, Christian. You always believe in me, want the best for me, and cheer me on. I love each of you very much, and I couldn't imagine life without you.

All pastors—May you invade your communities with reckless love and impact your cities with the life-changing message of Jesus. May you create an indispensable church, the kind of church about which even an atheist would say, "I don't believe what they believe, but I shudder at what would happen if they were no longer in our city. We need them!" Let's be that kind of church. Let's be those kinds of leaders. Let's go change the world!

can you imagine . . . ?

> The overriding character trait of Jesus is LOVE,
> and the entire Gospel story is woven with love.
> Sometimes it's not easy, and oftentimes it requires
> sacrifice, but it's when we love that we are the most
> like Jesus.
>
> —Steven Furtick

Can you imagine how attractive your church would be if people who had never gone to church before (or hadn't gone in a long time because they'd been turned off by painful past experiences) were direct recipients of your love, compassion, and tangible resources?

Can you imagine the reputation earned by your church when your people consistently show up when people are in need?

Can you imagine virtually everyone in the church getting their hands dirty by serving in every corner of the community—especially in places others don't want to go?

Can you imagine the mayor and city council seeing your pastor and others in your church as the most dependable, trustworthy, caring people in town?

Can you imagine the police and fire departments calling your church as their go-to option when they're helping people respond to a tragedy?

Can you imagine your church being woven so tightly into the fabric of the city that people throughout the community—including unbelievers—would be heartbroken if your church ceased to exist?

Can you imagine what a difference it would make if your church was known throughout your city for the genuine love your people have for each other?

Can you imagine how many people would want to come to your church if they were loved simply for who they are?

It can happen. In fact, it's already happening in churches throughout the country. It takes a little planning, a shot of creativity, some initiative on the part of leaders, and a willingness on the part of countless people to say, "Care for people in need? Count me in!"

In this book, I'll give you a taste of the ways churches have activated love to meet needs in their communities. Most churches that are part of this movement organize five to fifteen specific service projects on a couple of Saturdays twice a year. Individuals and families meet together for breakfast and then serve for about four hours. Among many other activities, they paint teachers' lounges at local schools, visit the elderly, provide resources for people who live on the streets, clean up for the Department of Parks and Rec, and partner with local nonprofits to do the things those organizations haven't had the time or resources to accomplish.

The Spark and the Fire

Let me go back to the beginning to explain how this movement started. In 2015, Dave Stewart, one of the campus pastors at the South Hills Church I lead, had an idea to get his church involved in a day of serving their community in Burbank, California. Dave and his leaders organized a few projects, and they were pleasantly surprised at the response. The people who participated thoroughly enjoyed diving in to care for people, and after a few of these one-day events, city leaders sat up and took notice. In addition, the enthusiasm of the people serving spilled over into every aspect of the life of the church. It appeared that volunteering on a Saturday for a few hours propelled a lot of people to serve in other capacities in the church. Also, they were motivated to give more generously to fund the serving events and the church's budget, and they were eager to reach out to their neighbors to tell them about Jesus.

At about the same time Dave told me about his campus's success in serving their community, I attended a conference and heard a tired line from thirty years ago: "If your church disappeared, would anyone in the community notice?" But when I heard it that time, it really hit me. In fact, I didn't think many people in our cities would notice if a lot of churches suddenly vanished. Instantly, I realized that what Dave and his church were doing was a powerful way to have an impact on a city—so they could be seen as an asset instead of a cipher. That moment was the spark . . . and then came the vision, the motivational fire, and the implementation.

I became a sponge to soak up everything Dave could tell me about how he was mobilizing and motivating his people to be involved in caring for people outside his church. We eventually launched these efforts at our eleven campuses. The impact was clear and powerful—on those we served and on our people. From there, the idea spread organically as I spoke about it at conferences; coached pastors through our coaching arm, Church BOOM; and had conversations with pastors and church leaders throughout the country. I'm not sure when someone came up with the label, but soon we called the effort "Love Where You Live."

Enthusiasm and creativity have been hallmarks of the movement. People want to make a difference, and it seems they're just waiting for someone to say, "Hey, come with me. Together we'll meet needs and warm hearts in the neighborhoods around us." This isn't a top-down strategy. Every person has a network of connections, so every person can offer suggestions about new ways to care for people.

I've noticed that people who have been touched by the heart of Jesus are eager for Him to use them to serve others. They just need the opportunity.

As I write this, I think about a conversation I had recently with four pastors in San Diego. They told me their churches are struggling to find ways to connect with people in their city to serve them and communicate the love of Jesus. After they explained their frustration, I smiled and told them, "I think I've got something for you." That's a snapshot of dozens of similar conversations I've had with church leaders across the country.

Love Where You Live has revolutionized how I see the impact of the church, and this movement, like all movements, has developed a life of its own. The more we've participated in this way of serving, the more it makes perfect sense. I've drawn two main conclusions. First, it seems very obvious: Isn't this what Jesus would do? Isn't this what Jesus did? In the Gospels, we see Him out in the community caring for people far more than we see Him in synagogues. He didn't wait for people to come to Him. If He was with us today, wouldn't He spend a lot of time with people who aren't in church—not to chastise them but to love them where they live?

Second, church leaders are always looking for a competitive edge. What makes their churches different and attractive? Today, bands, sound systems, lighting, and videos are standard equipment in most churches. They were new once, but no more. But if pastors lead their people to serve in the community, all of them will discover their unique contribution and their unique attraction. All leaders are looking for their USP: their ultimate strategic position. In other words, what will make their organization stand out? Why would someone choose them instead of one of the many other options? I'm convinced Love Where You Live (LWYL) is an ultimate strategic position for any church.

When I explained these two points to the pastors in San Diego, their eyes lit up. They know they aren't better speakers than other pastors near them, their bands aren't that much better, and the same is true for their lighting, creative arts, children's church, and everything else. The pastors said they don't know any churches that have established a reputation for caring for people outside the walls of their churches. But I do.

What kind of reputation? Churches that are using this method of outreach have very positive articles written about them in local papers; they receive awards; their leaders are asked to speak at civic events; and they get kind notes from school principals, mayors, city council members, hospital administrators, and leaders of nonprofit organizations. For any particular church, that kind of reputation may be much different, much better, and far more attractive than the one they have now.

Love Where You Live has become a movement because it inspires people to get involved in being the voice, hands, and feet of Jesus—and they realize they make a difference in their city. The people in our community are so grateful for our help, which, of course, reinforces our commitment to serve them again. I know one thing: I'll never go back to the old way of doing church.

Let me assure you, I'm not talking only about megachurches. In fact, most of the stories you'll read about in this book are from churches of one to three hundred people. Big churches have more people and more resources, but we've seen churches of every size make a big difference in the lives of people in their communities. In this movement, size really doesn't matter—it's all about heart.

A Glimpse of the Impact

The stories are endless, but let me begin with one of my favorites. When people in our churches get involved in actively loving people in our communities, they become sensitized to needs they hadn't noticed before. That's what happened to Bethany. One day she told Chris Bristow, pastor of The Ark Church in San Clemente, California, about a small hospital that cares for children who are victims of severe burns. The hospital's eight staff members display enormous tenderness and provide hope for these kids, and Bethany asked if the church could do something to honor them.

Chris met with the leadership team to tell them about Bethany's plan, and they thought it was a great idea. They talked and prayed and came up with a specific plan. A month or so later, Chris invited the hospital staff team to a worship service. That morning, he asked them to come to the platform, and he showed a video about the care they provide. Most of the people in the church had never even heard of this specialized hospital, and they were moved by the team's compassion for the kids. When the video ended, the people gave the hospital staff members a standing ovation.

> When people in our churches get involved in actively loving people in our communities, they become sensitized to needs they hadn't noticed before.

Before they went back to their seats, Chris asked them to wait a minute. He had secretly worked it out with their administrator to find replacements for them for a day, and the church gave them tickets to Disneyland for a surprise day off. Several of them had tears streaming down their faces. They had served in relative obscurity, day after day, to care for kids in excruciating pain—and for their very worried parents. This was a way for the people at the church to learn about them and show appreciation in a very tangible way. It happened because one person was moved with compassion and voiced an idea.

Dan Nalley, pastor of Church of the Harvest in Roseville, California, has a big heart for those who live on the streets, and the people in his church don't have to look very far to find them. Love Where You Live has become integral to the culture of that church. The people regularly go to the streets to provide food, blankets, and personal hygiene supplies to those who can't afford them. In one of these events, one of their teams passed out food and blankets to people living under a bridge. There, they met a woman—I'll call her Alicia—who was eager to take anything they offered because she had been using newspapers to stay warm at night. The team members connected with her, led her to Christ, and invited her to church. The next Sunday, Alicia walked in. Two of the people who had met her under the bridge recognized her and welcomed her. In the warmth of their love and security, Alicia found new hope, uncovered latent skills, got a job, found an apartment, and became part of the church's life.

People who are new to the church are often shocked to hear Alicia's story. They shouldn't be. Dan and the people of his church have lots of stories of God's love, power, and redemptive grace, often initiated by the church members and attenders who are willing to care for people who have given up hope.

Dan's church realized that people were going hungry every day, not just on the days they gathered food and supplies and teams went to the streets. They also offered lunches for hungry people who came to the church each day. One of these was a young man who didn't weigh more than ninety pounds and was strung out on drugs. He came every day for months, and then suddenly he stopped coming. No one knew what had happened to him.

On a Sunday morning a year and a half later, a very muscular young man sat in the front row and sang with all his heart. When Dan talked to him after the service, the man almost laughed as he said, "Don't you recognize me, Pastor?"

Dan shook his head. "No, I'm sorry, but I don't."

The man smiled. "You might remember a skinny guy who was on drugs and came here to eat every day." He waited a second for Dan to take a closer look. When Dan's eyes widened in surprise, he continued, "Yeah, it's me. I trusted in Jesus and moved to Alaska to go to rehab. Pastor, I had nothing and nobody, but your church loved me and fed me every single day. Without you, I'd still be on the street . . . or dead."

Pastor Nate Gagne leads Restoration Church in Dover, New Hampshire. In the cold winters of New England, Nate and his people have a unique outreach to love people in their community: "Boots and Socks." They collect and buy good boots and warm socks in children's sizes, and they knock on doors in the low-cost housing complexes in their city to distribute them. They met a single mom, Jen, whose daughter needed footwear, and the team invited Jen and her daughter to church. Jen was reluctant at first, but she decided to give it a try. She heard the Good News and trusted in Christ, and she began serving in the church. About eighteen months later, she was diagnosed with cancer and was given only a couple of months to live. She wanted to be baptized as soon as possible, and she invited about thirty of her unsaved friends to come to the service. Jen died only weeks later, but a number of her friends have become believers, and today they're active participants in the life of the church. One "Boots and Socks" connection has had an eternal impact on Jen, her daughter, and several of her friends. And of course, Jen's faith had a remarkable impact on the people in the church.

At Next Level Church in Hampton, Virginia, Pastor Rob Shepherd's community outreach took a different form. Instead of his people going into the neighborhoods to provide food for the hungry, they invited people to the church for a banquet. They went to the most disadvantaged neighborhoods to meet people and give personal invitations. The dinner was a first-class affair with catered food, tablecloths, nice plates and glasses, silverware, and flowers. The people who had given the invitations served as waitstaff. The room was packed, and the atmosphere was filled with a wonderful blend of excitement and love. The event made a big splash in the city, and it made an even bigger impact in the lives of people who felt seen, heard, and wanted—maybe for the first time in their lives.

I could tell many, many more stories, but you get the idea. As churches have LWYL Saturdays (or whatever day they're held), a couple of things invariably happen: those in the church get excited to work together to touch the lives of people, and the number of organizations that want the church's help gets so long that some have to be put on a waiting list. Leaders of nonprofits, school administrators, and government officials want to get in on all this love! It doesn't take long to develop a reputation as a church that moves beyond its walls to care for people in its community.

The Great Equalizer

As I've watched thousands of individuals and families partici-pate in Love Where You Live, one of the primary benefits I've noticed is that serving gets people out of their own world so they can experience, if only for a few hours, the genuine and often heartbreaking needs of others in their communities. Some would say they're getting out of their comfort zones. That's part of it, but I think it's more than that. Actually, people are getting out of their oblivion zones. Most of us have care-fully constructed our lives to be safe and secure and to avoid as much inconvenience as possible. That's completely understandable, but it's completely limiting—it insulates us from people Jesus loves . . . who are the people Jesus wants us to love.

Getting involved in meeting the needs of others has two immediate benefits:

1. Serving helps us see that people we don't normally interact with are real people with real hopes and dreams—people very much like us. They love their families like we do, they're searching for a better life like we are, and they want their lives to count like we do.

2. Serving also breaks down barriers between Christians. It's easy to cherish petty jealousies and hold grudges against each other, but it's much harder to have those feelings when you both have your sleeves rolled up and are holding shovels, wrenches, or paintbrushes. I've seen a corporate CEO working side by side with a lady who stocks shelves at Walmart. They may live in different parts of town, but for those hours on a Saturday, they serve together as peers.

Many leaders talk about creating unity in the church, but they don't do much to make it happen. Serving with others is, from

> It's easy to cherish petty jealousies and hold grudges against each other, but it's much harder to have those feelings when you both have your sleeves rolled up and are holding shovels, wrenches, or paintbrushes.

my observation, one of the most effective ways to create bonds between people in a church. No matter how different their backgrounds may be, they now have a shared experience. Then, when they see each other in church or at the grocery store, they don't just walk past each other. They stop and talk because they've joined hands and hearts in serving the community.

No Limits

I'm writing this book for a broad audience: pastors, church staff members, board members, volunteers, church attenders, and people who serve in nonprofit organizations. All of us have the privilege to represent Jesus in caring for those in need in our communities. Some of the applications I'll describe are for leaders as they cast the vision, plan, and gather resources, but most of the points apply to everyone. There are no limits on who can participate. All we need is a beating heart and a willingness to carve out time to pour love into some people.

Is this something you want to do? Let me ask you:

Do you feel the pain and emptiness of people who are struggling? That shows you're in touch with God's heart.

Do you want to be more excited about Jesus? Be the hands, feet, and voice of Jesus, and you'll never be the same.

Do you want to provide specific, tangible, meaningful care for people in your city? Mobilize people (and yourself) to serve outside the walls of the church.

Do you want to build stronger relationships in small groups and teams throughout your church? Invite people to serve together.

Do you want your church to have a reputation as a compassionate community? Reach into the recesses of your city to care for people who often feel neglected.

Do you want city leaders to see your church as a valuable asset? Serve them with no strings attached, expecting nothing in return.

Do you want your church to grow? Take people outside the church's walls to make a difference in the community.

Do you want to experience more of the love of Jesus? Share more of His love.

"Follow Me"

Jesus had a consistent message to people who were interested in Him. He invited four fishermen, a tax collector, a rebel, other disciples, a group of women, and all who were listening to "Come, follow Me." Where did He lead them? To meetings with the powerful and encounters with the powerless, to formal celebrations like a wedding and a "chance" encounter with a lonely woman drawing water, to those who lived nearby and those who lived across the country, to fellow Jews and to Romans and Samaritans, to comfortable and refreshing retreats and to crowded hillsides, to touch lepers who were the dregs of society and to have dinner with the richest man in town. When people followed Jesus, He took them places they would never have gone on their own, and He showed them what it meant to genuinely love the people they met there.

Jesus developed a reputation for being very different from the other religious leaders. Many followed Him out of curiosity, some were touched by His kindness and power, and a few despised Him because His popularity threatened their positions. The religious leaders harshly judged those who were struggling and blamed them for their troubles, but Jesus entered their world and loved them.

As Jesus' love for people became evident, His crowds grew. He began a small movement and gathered a few people around Him, and soon a lot of people wanted to see Him. He spoke to about twenty thousand people—and catered a miraculous meal for them.

Love attracts. The love of Jesus is wider, longer, deeper, and higher than anything people have ever experienced before.

> If you want your church to grow, follow Jesus to serve people in your community. Get outside the church. That's where Jesus went, that's where I'm going, and that's where I'm inviting you to go too.

They couldn't get enough then, and they can't get enough now. If you want your church to grow, follow Jesus to serve people in your community. Get outside the church. That's where Jesus went, that's where I'm going, and that's where I'm inviting you to go too.

A Choice, an Action, a Movement

What motivates us to be agents of change in our communities? What steps do we take?

1. *It's a choice.*

    Guilt makes us feel bad and pressures us to comply, but obeying God isn't about feeling guilty; it's about feeling responsible. Fear makes us insecure and desperate to please. Pride causes us to feel superior and powerful. Those feelings may prompt us to take action, but the action seldom lasts. And besides, those motivations are more about us than about the people in need—and of course, the latter category includes all of us at one time or another.

    Do you think people can tell when we treat them as problems to solve instead of human beings? Sure they can, and they resent it. Change happens when we reach out in love—and change begins inside us. Our hearts are transformed only when we experience the heart of Jesus. When His love, forgiveness, kindness, and acceptance become real to us, we choose to become agents of change. We're willing to go anywhere He leads us, and we're eager to love everyone He loves.

> When His love, forgiveness, kindness, and acceptance become real to us, we choose to become agents of change.

2. *It's an action.*

    Love is more than an emotion. Love takes action. It's embodied in attitudes, choices, and concrete steps to meet needs. But love always has a feedback loop.

    On the night Jesus was betrayed, before He died on the cross, He explained the connection between our experience of God's love and our willingness to follow: "Those who accept my commandments and obey them are the ones who love me. And because they love me, my Father will love them. And I will love them and reveal myself to each of them" (John 14:21). His command is to follow Him, and we obey by serving the people He loves. When we do, we sense more of God's love than ever before. That's His promise.

3. *It's a movement.*

Today, many people are skeptical of the church because we've misrepresented Jesus so badly by remaining passive in the face of suffering and hopelessness. But we have the opportunity to change their perception. When we involve our families, small groups, and teams in loving where we live, love multiplies for all of us. And as churches mobilize people to step into the cracks and crevices of our cities, as we serve the mayors and the homeless, as we partner with organizations that are doing great work to help them do even more, and as our churches become known as channels of Jesus' love, amazing things will happen. Strained and broken relationships will be healed, despairing people will find hope, overlooked people will feel included and honored, generosity will meet real needs, and countless people will want to know more about the Jesus who prompted all of this. And as Jesus promised, we'll have a new sense of wonder and gratitude that He loves us so much.

When we make the choice, engage in the action, and propel the movement, who will be changed? All of us.

You may be a church attender who wants to move outside your normal range of relationships to make a difference. You may be a leader of a small group or team who wants your people to experience the joy of working together to change lives. You may be a pastor who wants your church's reputation to be profoundly positive in the eyes of city leaders and people throughout the community.

Love Where You Live movements change us as individuals. They also change our teams and groups, our churches, our neighborhoods, and our communities. Every act of compassion, every moment we serve, and every resource we invest to care for others points to Jesus, the King who stooped to serve you and me.

At the end of each chapter, you'll find a few questions and prayers designed to stimulate personal reflection and application. Don't rush through these. You don't get extra credit for speed! Take time to pray about and consider how you can apply the lessons from each chapter. Also, use the questions with your spouse, your family, your friends, and your small group to explore how you can be more effective as you touch lives outside the walls of your church.

THINK ABOUT IT

1. How do you think most church attenders would answer this question: "If your church disappeared, would anyone in the community notice?" What's your answer? Why?

2. Describe the pattern of Jesus' life. How much time did He spend with insiders, and how often did He

move into the lives of people in the communities where He traveled? Are there any scenes in the Gospels that particularly make this point? What happened in them?

3. What do you hope to get out of this book?

PRAY ABOUT IT

Ask God to use your reading and reflection to give you a clear picture of how He wants to use you in your community.

DO IT

You'll have plenty of opportunities to take action later in the study, but at this point, just keep reading.

love is a verb

> Love is never stationary in the end. Love doesn't just keep thinking about it or keep planning for it. Simply put: love does!
>
> —Bob Goff, *Love Does*

A man I'll call Jack regularly attended Family Church in Whittier, California, but from his normal expression, it would be hard to say he experienced much of God's joy. Behind his scowl was a hardened man. When he was a boy, his alcoholic father walked out on the family. Jack had tried to create a loving family of his own, but it hadn't worked. He had been married and divorced twice, and some of the wounds were still open and raw. His third marriage was on the rocks, and he was desperate. He decided to try church as a possible solution. He may have thought love would enter his heart by osmosis, but the message of grace bounced off like it was water hitting concrete. During the year and a half Jack attended, the church conducted three Love Where You Live outreaches, but he didn't get involved.

When people invited him to join their teams, he invariably growled, "I don't have time for that." Once, after an awkward moment of silence, he muttered angrily, "I give my offering. Isn't that enough?"

When the next Love Where You Live Saturday approached, another person invited him to join a team. (Maybe he didn't know Jack had turned down so many others, so he wasn't shy about asking him!) This time Jack agreed to go. The next Saturday, he showed up at the church in his work clothes. The team drove to a group home for developmentally challenged children. They grabbed buckets of paint, brushes, rollers, and drop cloths to spruce up the main meeting room.

During the day, some of the kids wanted to talk to Jack. They gravitated toward him because he's a big, muscular man—they may have thought he was a version of the Incredible Hulk! Jack took time to engage with these kids, and that day God did something wonderful to melt his hardened heart. A few weeks later, he reflected, "Man, it was awful. My bitterness was destroying me. I had become completely self-absorbed in my resentments. That day, I saw children who had far fewer resources than me, but they were happy. In fact, they were happy to interact *with me*! I realize now that I can get out of myself by showing some love to others, and in loving them, God is doing something powerful to heal me. I don't understand it, but I love it."

A year later, Jack was invited to be a team leader for Love Where You Live Saturdays. He asked if his team could go back to the group home where the miracle of love began for him. He and his team cleaned up the grounds, planted flowers, and did several maintenance projects . . . and of course, they spent time loving the kids. For Jack, taking action to love others was the key to his experience of God's powerful, healing love.

His Very Nature

We live in the information age, but it appears that we've spread a lot of misinformation about the characteristics of God. One of the most obnoxious descriptions is found in the film *Talladega Nights: The Ballad of Ricky Bobby*. At dinner with his buddy Cal, Ricky Bobby prays, "Dear eight-pound, six-ounce, newborn baby Jesus, in your golden, fleece diapers, with your curled-up, fat, balled-up little fists pawin' at the air—"

"He was a man! He had a beard!" Cal interrupts.

Ricky Bobby insists, "I like the baby version the best, do you hear me?"[1]

> We live in the information age, but it appears that we've spread a lot of misinformation about the characteristics of God.

Whether we laugh or are offended, the point is that we tend to create God the way we want Him, or perhaps the way we fear He might be. Some people imagine God as a harsh judge or a policeman lying in wait to catch them doing something wrong. Others see Him as a kind but mildly senile grandfather who means well but doesn't really know what's going on in our lives. Many assume that it's God's primary job to make our lives pleasant and meaningful, and if He doesn't, He's not worth following.

The Bible gives us a very different picture of God. He is a God of perfect love *and* perfect justice—at the same time. We tend to focus on one and discount the other. How can God hold both together? Because of our sins, we deserve God's righteous judgment, but in His infinite love, Jesus took our punishment. He takes the initiative. We often hear Jesus' words to Nicodemus, a religious leader: "For this is how God loved the world: He gave his one and only Son, so that everyone who believes in him will not perish but have eternal life" (John 3:16). We get another angle on the nature of God in John's first letter:

> But anyone who does not love does not know God, for God is love.
>
> God showed how much he loved us by sending his one and only Son into the world so that we might have eternal life through him. This is real love—not that we loved God, but that he loved us and sent his Son as a sacrifice to take away our sins. (1 John 4:8–10)

God doesn't *try* to love. He *is* love. It's His very nature to love, and not just to love those who are lovely or who can repay Him. He loves even the unlovely and those who have nothing to give back. Our love for people is often conditional, but God's love is *counterconditional*—in spite of our condition of being undeserving. That's why it's called grace: undeserved favor, love, kindness, and rescue. We can choose to love or to withhold love, but love is at the heart of who God is. He always loves.

What's the nature of love? It's sacrificial. It gives until it hurts, and it gives some more. The measure of God's love is the cross of Jesus. That's where we see infinite love demonstrated by a perfect and happy being sacrificing himself for passive, selfish, defiant, and clueless people. People like me and—no offense—people like you.

As John points out, it's inconceivable that anyone would claim to know God and not love Him and the people He loves—which is every person on the planet. John draws the obvious conclusion: "Dear friends, since God loved us that much, we surely ought to love each other" (v. 11).

> What's the nature of love? It's sacrificial. It gives until it hurts, and it gives some more.

We get the clearest picture of God when we look at Jesus. The writer of Hebrews explains, "[God] has spoken to us through his Son. God promised everything to the Son as an inheritance, and through the Son he created the universe. The Son radiates God's own glory and expresses the very character of God, and he sustains everything by the mighty power of his command" (1:2–3). When we read the accounts of Matthew, Mark, Luke, and John, we get a glimpse of the heart of Jesus.

Many years ago, a pastor named B. B. Warfield wrote an article called "The Emotional Life of Our Lord." As he read the Gospels, he noticed that the four writers described one of Jesus' emotions more than all the others combined: His compassion. Again and again, Jesus felt an "internal movement of pity," which prompted "an external act of beneficence"—a specific act of love.[2]

Jesus hasn't changed since the four writers described His amazing love for people. He still has compassion for people who are sick, discouraged, helpless, bitter, and hopeless. But today, He puts His compassionate heart into us, and He has given us the privilege of representing Him to the people in our communities. God gave the Spirit of Jesus to live inside us so we can react with compassion when we see the needs of people, and we can respond with tangible, specific actions to meet those needs. Love is God's nature, and love becomes our nature too.

Let me put it another way: God never decides that He won't be loving, and if we know Him at all, our experience of His love will prompt us to notice needs and take action to meet them. As we experience the love of Jesus, we'll gradually become more like Him.

Getting His Hands Dirty

Jesus didn't stay in a comfortable setting and just teach people about love. He didn't post cool sayings about love on social media and check to see how many likes He got. Jesus went to people and, as we've seen, often to places where other leaders wouldn't go. He went out of His way to spend time with a Samaritan woman, and as John makes clear in his account of this story, the Jews hated the Samaritans, so Jesus broke rigid social barriers. He touched lepers and people who were crippled and blind, and since physical problems were interpreted as spiritual problems, others considered Him to be "unclean" when He touched them, so Jesus broke religious barriers. He responded to the plea of a Roman officer to heal his servant, and the Romans were despised as an occupying force, so Jesus broke political barriers. Jesus was willing (I think we can even say eager) to demonstrate exuberant love for people at the risk of His reputation. In fact, the religious leaders were so upset with Him that from the earliest days of His ministry, they tried to discredit Him and even kill Him.

One of my favorite moments in the Gospels is found in John. Jesus had come to the temple in Jerusalem to tell the crowd about God's love.

> As he was speaking, the teachers of religious law and the Pharisees brought a woman who had been caught in the act of adultery. They put her in front of the crowd.
>
> "Teacher," they said to Jesus, "this woman was caught in the act of adultery. The law of Moses says to stone her. What do you say?" (John 8:3–5)

They thought they had Him! If He said, "Stone her," they could accuse Him of not being as loving as He claimed. If He said, "Don't stone her," they could accuse Him of not being faithful to the laws God had given them.

He didn't take the bait.

> Jesus stooped down and wrote in the dust with his finger. They kept demanding an answer, so he stood up again and said, "All right, but let the one who has never sinned throw the first stone!" Then he stooped down again and wrote in the dust. (vv. 6–8)

Talk about getting your hands dirty! We don't know what Jesus wrote in the dust that day. It may have been something about the woman's sins, or it may have been a list of the leaders' sins. Whatever it was, it was written in dust, and with one swipe of His hand, He could erase it with His love and forgiveness.

Jesus' actions completely changed the atmosphere of the moment.

> When the accusers heard this, they slipped away one by one, beginning with the oldest, until only Jesus was left in the middle of the crowd with the woman. Then Jesus stood up again and said to the woman, "Where are your accusers? Didn't even one of them condemn you?"
> "No, Lord," she said.
> And Jesus said, "Neither do I. Go and sin no more." (vv. 9–11)

I wish I could have been there to see the look on everyone's faces! The woman had faced certain death. The religious leaders treated her with contempt, but Jesus treated her with the utmost kindness and grace. The leaders were sure they had Jesus in their trap, but their confidence turned to embarrassment when He wrote in the dust. The disciples may have wondered if the leaders had finally put Jesus in a bind, and they must have laughed with relief when the woman was left alone in front of Jesus. He stepped into the awkward, threatening scene and loved the person others had already judged and were ready to execute.

> Jesus stepped into the awkward, threatening scene and loved the person others had already judged and were ready to execute.

First Things First

When people trust in Christ, we look for steps of faith. Most of the time, we're happy when they come back to church, and we're ecstatic if they join a small group! Most of us are content to leave people in a comfortable place worshiping in the church, but that's not Jesus' strategy of discipleship. Matthew gives us a shocking sequence: "Jesus called his twelve disciples together and gave them authority to cast out evil spirits and to heal every kind of disease and illness" (Matt. 10:1). What? From the beginning, Jesus took the disciples out of their comfort zones and sent them out to make a difference in the lives of needy people. How needy? These people were demon-possessed and had every kind of sickness known to humankind. How's this for a training tip: "Go and announce to them that the Kingdom of Heaven is near. Heal the sick, raise the dead, cure those with leprosy, and cast out demons. Give as freely as you have received!" (vv. 7–8).

Our strategy is different. We expect people to come for months or even years, to learn to give, and eventually to serve in some way, almost always inside the church. After a few years, they might attend a class on discipleship, but even then, we don't expect them to take dramatic action to change the world around them. The loud and clear message is, "Hey, watch the professionals serve God. Maybe someday you can do something significant, but there's no hurry." I'm afraid we've made people into passive critics instead of passionate disciples.

Our Inner Pharisee

The Gospels depict a stark contrast between Jesus and the religious leaders. The main group that despised Jesus was the Pharisees. They come across as narrow, rigid, and spiteful, but they were actually the good guys in Roman-occupied Palestine. When the nation was under foreign domination, they tried to keep the traditions alive. They were, though, far too zealous for their traditions and not in touch with the heart of God.

The Pharisees were the most powerful group in the Jewish culture. They had the respect of the people, but it was respect born of fear, not love. They enjoyed privileged positions, and they refused to stoop low enough to care for people in need—people who the Pharisees were sure were beneath them. Jesus tried to convince them that God wants more than compliance with rigid rules; He wants our hearts. When they continued to defy Him, Jesus wasn't shy about calling them out:

> What sorrow awaits you teachers of religious law and you Pharisees. Hypocrites! For you are careful to tithe even the tiniest income from your herb gardens, but you ignore the more important aspects of the law—justice, mercy, and faith. You should tithe, yes, but do not neglect the more important things. (Matt. 23:23).

The Pharisees despised Jesus for being so different:

- They loved power. Jesus was vulnerable and identified with the weak.
- They delighted in judging people. Jesus delighted in loving people.
- They compared themselves with others and felt superior. Jesus was criticized for caring for misfits and outcasts.
- They separated themselves from "those people." Jesus always moved toward "those people."

- They created a world in which they demanded respect. Jesus loved people enough to risk His reputation, His safety, and His life.

We want to ask, "What's the deal? Why didn't the Pharisees see themselves and Jesus more clearly?" The answer is a stark truth, not just for them but for all of us: people see only what they're prepared to see. We're often willfully blind to truths that challenge our existing biases.

So, who are you and I in the story? Are we more like the Pharisees or more like Jesus? Do we sit back in our comfortable place and ignore the people God loves because caring for them is inconvenient, or do we move toward them, pay a price in time and resources, and treat them like people Jesus dearly loves?

> People see only what they're prepared to see.

Too often, we consider what's in our hands "ours," so we believe we have complete control over how we use our resources. We need to realize that everything—everything—we have comes from the hand of our generous God. We don't share our resources with Him; He shares them with us.

I'm afraid we exhaust ourselves in church activities that are decidedly secondary, and we fail in the single most important role God has given us: to love people as He loves us—gladly, sacrificially, compassionately, and effectively.

Love is very fragile. It can be destroyed by an unkind word, eroded by neglect, or shattered by abuse. However, it thrives when people are well aware of their flaws, experience the forgiveness and love of God, and become channels of His love into the lives of those around them.

God leaves it to us to respond to His great love. He spoke and created the universe, and Jesus demonstrated power over wind, waves, demons, and sickness, but He doesn't force us to love Him. He lets us choose our response to Him. More than anything, He wants a loving relationship with us, so He never bullies, and He never uses guilt to manipulate us. He simply says, "I'm love. I'm the Good Shepherd. I'm your greatest hope. Come to Me." And He lets us move toward Him, move away from Him, or stay stuck in neutral.

Easy Steps

I'm convinced we can add value to people's lives by taking some easy, simple steps. I don't know how I developed this habit, but when I travel and go to the restroom at the airport, if the janitor is there, I make a point to look him in the eye and say something like, "Hey, thank you for what you do for me and everybody who comes in here. You're doing a great job, and I appreciate it." Invariably, my words induce a big smile. Even if the guy doesn't speak English, my tone of voice and the look on my face probably speak more clearly than my words.

It doesn't take much to move toward people and enter their world for a few seconds. Many people desperately need someone—anyone!—to show some appreciation or even just to acknowledge their existence.

Love is a verb. Get moving.

If I can do it, you can do it. Love is a verb. Get moving.

THINK ABOUT IT

1. Look back at the opening story about Jack. What's the "magic" that can happen in a person—even an angry, bitter person—who gets actively involved in loving people?

2. What are some common misconceptions about God? How do each of them short-circuit the experience of God's love?

3. Do you agree or disagree with the statement "Compassion inevitably produces loving action"? Why?

4. What are some reasons it's important to get people involved in loving others from the first days they trust in Jesus? What happens when they don't get involved that early?

5. Do you know any people in your church or small group who act like Pharisees? (No names, please!) What are some things you have to watch out for as you move away from your inner Pharisee to love like Jesus?

PRAY ABOUT IT

Ask God to show you any inclination you have toward being a Pharisee. When He shows you (and He almost certainly will), thank Him for His forgiveness and trust Him to give you more of a heart like Jesus.

DO IT

Each day for the next week, take a few seconds to speak words of appreciation to people in your world, possibly including:

- a waiter or waitress
- a salesperson
- a delivery person
- a cashier
- a neighbor
- a coworker
- your spouse
- your kids

3

my neighbor

God teaches us to love by putting some unlovely
people around us. It takes no character to love
people who are lovely and loving to you.

—Rick Warren

Brad and his wife, Catherine, were in their midthirties. They
had lived in their neighborhood for a couple of years, but they
hadn't developed more than superficial relationships with most
of the people living near them. They heard from their next-
door neighbor that the couple across the street had blown up
their marriage. The husband, they discovered, had left home
a week before, leaving his wife—Judith, they remembered—
with two little children to raise on her own.

The next Saturday morning, Brad noticed Judith washing
her car and trying to keep her five-year-old and three-year-
old corralled and out of the street. When Catherine walked
outside, they both watched her. Brad said, "We need to do
something. I'm not sure what, but something."

A few days later, Brad saw a lawn service truck and trailer pull up to the house next to Judith's. He thought they might be there to cut her grass, but they finished the house next to hers and drove away. The next Saturday, he saw Judith trying to start her mower, still attempting to keep an eye on her two little ones.

Brad realized this was his chance to step in to help. He opened his garage door, took out his lawn mower, and walked across the street. He had introduced himself months before, but he wasn't sure she would remember his name, so he told her, "Hey, you may not remember me. I'm Brad from across the street." She smiled weakly. He told her, "Don't worry about your grass. I've got it." He didn't wait for a response. He pulled the cord and the mower roared to life. She rolled her mower into her garage and sat with her children on her front steps as they watched Brad go back and forth.

Every Saturday morning for the next several months, Brad cut his grass and then walked across the street to mow Judith's. She tried several times to tell him he didn't have to do it, but he assured her that he was glad to. He and Catherine had quite a few good conversations with her, and they offered to watch the children when she had a doctor's appointment.

A few weeks later, she and her kids walked into church with Brad and Catherine. That morning, Judith gave her life to Christ.

Two Laws, One Heart

We've already taken a quick look at a powerful group of leaders in Jesus' day, the Pharisees. They were always looking for ways to make Him appear foolish. In Luke's account of the life of Christ, he puts us in a scene where an expert in the Jewish law asked what seemed to be a sincere question: "Teacher, what should I do to inherit eternal life?" (Luke 10:25).

But it was a trick. The Bible of that day, the part we call the Old Testament (because the New Testament about Jesus hadn't been written yet), contained 613 specific commands from God. The law expert wanted to see if Jesus would pick one so they could accuse Him of discounting all the rest, or if Jesus would be so baffled by the question that He couldn't answer it. Yet Jesus, the master teacher, turned the question around.

> Jesus replied, "What does the law of Moses say? How do you read it?"
>
> The man answered, "'You must love the LORD your God with all your heart, all your soul, all your strength, and all your mind.' And, 'Love your neighbor as yourself.'"
>
> "Right!" Jesus told him. "Do this and you will live!" (vv. 26–28)

The man realized that love was the preeminent law, the most important principle in the universe, the standard by which everything is measured, and the way we encounter the wonder of God's presence and purpose. Jesus was thrilled the man had answered correctly.

The guy should have stopped while he was ahead, but he didn't. He stuck his foot in his mouth. Luke tells us, "The man wanted to justify his actions, so he asked Jesus, 'And who is my neighbor?'" (v. 29).

This was a heavily weighted question. In the Bible, to be "justified" means to be made right with God. It has always involved faith in God's forgiveness, but the law expert wanted Jesus to affirm that his behavior had scored big points with God. When he asked, "Who is my neighbor?" he was trying to limit the scope of his love. He had hoped (and maybe expected) Jesus would say, "Oh, only faithful Jews—the ones just like you. They're the only ones God wants you to love. Does that work for you?" The man would have responded, "I'm good with that!"

> Jesus wasn't interested in limiting the scope of the love we show others.

But Jesus wasn't interested in limiting the scope of the love we show others. He blew the man's expectations to shreds by telling him a story, and each character in the story played a crucial part in the lesson Jesus was imparting. He began:

> A Jewish man was traveling from Jerusalem down to Jericho, and he was attacked by bandits. They stripped him of his clothes, beat him up, and left him half dead beside the road. By chance a priest came along. But when he saw the man lying there, he crossed to the other side of the road and passed him by. A Temple assistant walked over and looked at him lying there, but he also passed by on the other side. (vv. 30–32)

A Jewish man was, in that society, at the top of the social ladder. He had status in his family and in the community. This man was traveling, presumably on business, when he was attacked and robbed, leaving him near death on the side of the road. Priests were the guardians of the temple, the ones

50

who represented God to people and people to God. If anyone was expected to follow God's command to love his neighbor, it was a priest. In Jesus' story, the priest should have jumped in to help, but instead, he stayed as far away as possible and didn't let the man's condition delay him at all. Then a temple assistant did the same thing. These two men should have been first off the EMS truck to care for their countryman, but they were too busy, too distracted, too scared, or too hard-hearted to stop to help. Jesus' point is clear: the ones who should have loved the broken and bloody man didn't lift a finger to help him—a man whose condition wasn't his own fault; he was the victim of a crime.

But that's not the end of the story. Jesus shocked the law expert and everyone else who was listening when He told them:

> Then a despised Samaritan came along, and when he saw the man, he felt compassion for him. Going over to him, the Samaritan soothed his wounds with olive oil and wine and bandaged them. Then he put the man on his own donkey and took him to an inn, where he took care of him. The next day he handed the innkeeper two silver coins, telling him, "Take care of this man. If his bill runs higher than this, I'll pay you the next time I'm here." (vv. 33–35)

Lessons the Samaritan Teaches Us

The Jews had made a national sport of hating people from Samaria. The Samaritans were people who had a mixed heritage—they were descendants of Jews who had married Gentiles hundreds of years before. They were outcasts from the Jewish nation, so they developed their own form of worship and lived in separate communities. If you think the Republicans and Democrats can't stand each other, you haven't seen anything like the hatred between the Jews and the Samaritans!

That's why it was stunning that the hero of Jesus' story was a Samaritan. And what a hero! We learn four lessons by observing him:

1. He didn't stop to care for the man out of empty obligation—he had compassion for him.
2. He didn't give the minimum of care—he tenderly administered first aid on the spot.
3. He wasn't stingy—he paid for the man's care at the inn, and he promised to pay any additional expenses until the man got well.
4. He did all this for a Jewish man who never would have given him the time of day.

Loving our neighbor as ourselves doesn't have racial, social, or economic limits. It means that we notice when others close their eyes to people in need, we stop when others walk by, we get involved when others don't bother, and we're generous when others protect their wallets.

I love how this scene ends. Jesus asked the law expert to give his analysis of the point of the story:

> "Now which of these three would you say was a neighbor to the man who was attacked by bandits?" Jesus asked.
>
> The man replied, "The one who showed him mercy." (vv. 36–37)

His answer was accurate and enlightening. He was right that the Samaritan was the only one who had loved the victim and cared for him, but the law expert couldn't bring himself to say the word "Samaritan."

Jesus told him, "Yes, now go and do the same" (v. 37).

The Hero and the Villains

Who is the hero of the story? It was the most unlikely person, the one who had the best reason to walk away. The Samaritan crossed the street to care for the Jewish man. He crossed the line of racism, he crossed the line of inconvenience, he crossed the line of time, he crossed the line of cost, and he crossed the line of his reputation. His love was costly, but he gave it generously, with no complaints and no demands to be repaid.

Who are the villains? The ones who valued comfort and convenience, the ones who had more important work to do in the temple and couldn't afford to become "unclean" by touching a man who was bleeding. They had a lot of excuses (cleverly disguised as good reasons) to avoid the man in need, and they didn't have an ounce of love for him.

From countless conversations with people, I think a lot of us who go to church are like the law expert. We hear God say our first priority is to love Him and love people, and we say, "Got it. No problem. I love God and I love people." But we instinctively limit our love to the people who are close by, who are safe, and who don't ask too much. (I'm not trying to be rude, just honest.) If we're painfully honest, most of us are far more like the priest and the temple assistant than the Samaritan. We've packed our schedules so tight that we don't have time to stop and care for people; we've insulated ourselves from at least some of the needs in others' lives; we've concluded that it costs too much time, energy, and money to help people with sticky problems; and we don't want to be "unclean" by getting our hands dirty in their difficult and seemingly intractable troubles. We consider ourselves to be insiders, and we feel superior to those we see as outsiders.

> We instinctively limit our love to the people who are close by, who are safe, and who don't ask too much.

To use different terminology, we believe we're worthy, but we see those not like us as unworthy. Perhaps the biggest mistake is our assumption that what we're already "doing for God" by going to church a couple of times a month is "enough"—we've done our part, paid our dues, and sacrificed plenty.

I hope this description of you and your commitment to love like Jesus is completely wrong. Is it?

Starting from Behind

To be fair, some of us start with big deficits. Instead of growing up in environments of affirming love, we've suffered in homes that were characterized by violence, silence, ignorance, or absence:

- *Violence.* Abuse comes in many forms, including sexual, physical, and emotional. Depending on the age of the victim, the severity and frequency of the abuse, the absence of any protector, and the sensitivity of the victim, the person often suffers devastating impacts, including post-traumatic stress. The victim's reactions to this kind of violence can range from utter compliance to avoid the persecutor's rage; to becoming hardened and tough to avoid any hint of vulnerability; to escaping into drugs, alcohol, and sex; to engaging in any other diversion to keep from feeling the pain.

- *Silence.* In some ways, the wounds from emotional abandonment can be harder to heal than actual blows. The hurt is just as deep, but there are no bruises, no sneering faces, and nothing to connect the hurt with the cause.

- *Ignorance.* Some parents have never seen a healthy, loving home, so they don't know how to provide one. They often try their best, but they haven't internalized the blend of love and limits that every child needs.

- *Absence.* The hurt created by physical abandonment leaves a large crater of self-doubt. The person left behind instinctively wonders how they could be so deficient that a parent wouldn't love them enough to stay. Children don't have the intellectual and emotional capacity to make rational observations about the defectiveness of the parent who leaves. Instead, all the blame and shame turn inward.

Of course, many families contain a blend of these problems. A friend of mine recalls his childhood in a home where his father was a depressed, sometimes explosive alcoholic, and his mother was a control freak. ("A perfect match," he said.) The first time his father told him he loved him was when he was thirty years old. By this time, his dad had been diagnosed with late-stage pancreatic cancer and had stopped drinking.

When his mind cleared, he could express the affection my friend had longed to hear all his life. A couple of months later, his father died.

"Those last months were a gift from God," he related to me. "A lot of healing happened between my father and me, but the damage was deep." He has tried hard to show love to his wife and two children, to express love like his father couldn't, and to avoid repeating the oppressive control he endured from his mother.

Many of us have similar stories. The names and problems are different, but the effects are the same: we have difficulty giving and receiving love.

God has made children to be sponges, soaking up the environment around them. If their parents were loving, strong, and consistent, the kids soaked up those traits and become secure and able to give and receive love. But if the children lived in a chaotic family, they feel very insecure and desperate for love. Part of the healing process for people who grew up in these families is to become objective, to forgive, and to limit any further damage. Just because someone has *position* in your life doesn't mean they have *passage* to your life.

> Just because someone has *position* in your life doesn't mean they have *passage* to your life.

The promise of the gospel is that all of us can experience God's love more deeply than we ever imagined possible, and His love will transform us—maybe not immediately, and certainly not completely in this life. But our experience of God's love will enable us to take huge steps to love other people, if only we'll let it.

Three Walls

The man who wanted to narrow the scope of "neighbors" built walls to keep people out, but Jesus continually broke down walls to invite people in. Make no mistake: the walls are already there, and they're getting higher. It's human nature to look around and categorize people into insiders and outsiders. The people we let inside are those who talk like us, think like us, believe like us, eat like us, and cheer for the same baseball team. Everyone else is, by definition, an outsider.

We tend to exclude people because of three primary prejudices: race, social status, and politics. Overtly or subtly, many of us have erected walls to keep insiders in and outsiders out. Exclusion can have many different faces, including genuinely despising a group of people, being nice but paternalistic because we feel superior, and ignoring them and their needs. Let's look at these common prejudices:

- *Race.* Many people assumed racism wouldn't be a factor after the advances in the civil rights movement and the election of the first African American president, but in recent years it has raised its ugly head again. We can identify the "hard racism" of the skinheads, neo-Nazis, and other white nationalists, but we can also see plenty of "soft racism" in people's words—and their dismissive tone—as they talk about those with skin colors, ethnicities, and national origins different from their own.

- *Social status.* Throughout history, people with means have traditionally looked at the poor as ignorant, irresponsible, and generally "less than." This was featured in the class distinctions on the hit PBS series *Downton Abbey*, but it still happens even today in the assumption that people are poor only because they have a defective character—they're not smart enough, responsible enough, or productive enough to make it financially or socially.

- *Politics.* The discourse about political views has become incredibly heated and polarized, not just since 2020 but in the last fifteen to twenty years. In the past, opponents in Congress could argue their differing points and then have dinner as friends, but that's very rare today. And the rest of us have been caught up in the assumption that people on the other side of every issue are both evil and foolish. This wall has spikes and concertina wire!

The emotions about outsiders aren't always intense and off the charts. We may not despise "those people" the way Jews and Samaritans despised each other, but we may feel completely fine about not having anything to do with them. We may not move toward them in any meaningful way. We may keep our distance and hope they keep theirs. But if we move toward them to befriend them, how will we respond if our friends ridicule us? What if they exclude us and consider us unacceptable? Are we willing to pay the price? Jesus wants insiders to make sacrifices to make it easy for outsiders to come in.

Lessons for You and Me

Does the courage to address racism, social status, and politics have anything to do with Christians and the church? You bet it does! Far too often we're swept up in this us-against-them perspective, anger drives us apart so that we don't even listen to opposing views, and we spend time only with people who already agree with us. The world's values tell us to fiercely defend our rights because "people are out to get us." The threat is usually far more perceived than real, but perception determines our response: we conclude that life isn't fair, we're getting a raw deal, and we're afraid things will only get worse. Our goal, then, is self-protection. This negative view of life inevitably leads to a sense of entitlement—"I deserve better than this"—which causes even well-to-do people to feel like victims. This way of thinking produces resentment, not love. It echoes the law expert's question, "Who is my neighbor?" And for many, the answer is, "Those who look like me, believe like me, think like me, live where I live, and value what I value—and nobody else."

> What you don't value, you violate.

The priest and the temple assistant valued their convenience over the man lying on the side of the road. They demonstrated a clear principle: what you don't value, you violate.

That's not the lesson of the parable of the good Samaritan! Jesus calls Republicans to love Democrats and Democrats to love Republicans, Blacks and Whites and Browns to have compassion for each other, and rich and poor to see each other as equally valuable.

Before you run to your computer to send me a nasty email because you don't like what you've just read, let me assure you that what I'm saying is the heart of Jesus' message in this parable. It's too easy to watch news programs and listen to friends who pour gas on the fires of resentment. It's time to listen again to Jesus, and maybe really hear Him for the first time. When we're honest about people we've excluded from the category of neighbors, we need to remember that love covers a multitude of sins—their and ours.

Loving "the other" has to be more than rhetoric or good intentions. A pastor called to give me a report about a LWYL Saturday outreach in his community. He said that a week after the outreach, a lady came to his church because she had experienced love from one of the teams they had sent out. She came alone because she had no friends. She was new to the church (and to any church), but during the service the pastor could tell God was touching her heart. It was obvious she felt His loving presence, but before the service was over, she got up and walked out.

After the service, he saw her standing in the lobby. He introduced himself, and she bubbled over with excitement. She told him how members of a Love Where You Live team had shown her more love than she had ever felt in her life, and she asked them why they were caring for her. They explained that they're Christians and invited her to church. They had no idea that she would actually show up, but there she was.

The pastor asked her if something had bothered her during the service. It took her a few seconds to realize he was asking why she had left in the middle of worship, and she explained that she had gone to the restroom to flush vials of crack down the toilet. She then smiled and told him, "Today, I realized my worth. Because of Jesus, I'm not a nobody anymore." She paused for a second and then said, "I don't want to live that life ever again. I have a new life now."

Today, there is an epidemic of substance abuse and of other forms of addiction. A recent report by the US Surgeon General states that "over 27 million people in the United States reported current use of illicit drugs or misuse of prescription drugs, and over 66 million people (nearly a quarter of the adult and adolescent population) reported binge drinking in the past month."[1] This doesn't include other forms of addictive behavior involving tobacco, sex, food, gambling, exercise, and work.

The people who struggle with substance and behavior addictions aren't living on some other planet. We rub shoulders with them every day. For instance, there are "functional" alcoholics in many families and in virtually every neighborhood. Their drinking causes relational, financial, and career problems, but they manage to keep things together to some degree. True addicts typically are more out of control, harder to help, and cause enormous wreckage for themselves and everyone they touch.

It's hard enough to love a functional alcoholic, and most of us instinctively guard ourselves from the impact crater caused by addicts. But they are our neighbors too. Loving them isn't easy, and it may not be instantly productive, but sometimes God uses our attempts to love them to bring someone out of darkness and into the light of His grace.

Upside Down

I have a lot of patience with Jesus' disciples . . . because I have to admit that I'm so much like them! They were slow to understand what Jesus tried over and over again to communicate to them. To be fair, His lessons were diametrically different from anything they'd heard before. In other words, Jesus was introducing a kingdom that was upside down from what they expected. We get a glimpse of this in Mark's Gospel. Time after time, Jesus explained that He was going to be killed. He gave the disciples details about how it would happen, and He promised that He would experience a miraculous resurrection. But they didn't get it.

Right after one of these moments of self-revelation from Jesus, two brothers, James and John, asked Him if they could sit at the most prominent places next to him when He became king—which they expected to happen very soon. (Then, as now, proximity to power was an important status symbol, and the brothers wanted people to see their importance.) I can imagine Jesus shaking His head. They had completely missed the point! His kingdom would be characterized by service, not power; by kindness, not intimidation; by love, not fear. Jesus told them, "You don't know what you are asking! Are you able to drink from the bitter cup of suffering I am about to drink? Are you able to be baptized with the baptism of suffering I must be baptized with?" (Mark 10:38).

They still didn't have a clue. "'Oh yes,' they replied, 'we are able!'" (v. 39).

The other disciples overheard this conversation, and they missed the message too. They were furious that the two brothers were jockeying for the highest positions in the coming kingdom. I can almost hear them: "Who do James and John think they are?"

Jesus gathered all of them to set them straight:

You know that the rulers in this world lord it over their people, and officials flaunt their authority over those under them. But among you it will be different. Whoever wants to be a leader among you must be your servant, and whoever wants to be first among you must be the slave of everyone else. For even the Son of Man came not to be served but to serve others and to give his life as a ransom for many. (vv. 42–45)

That's the point: "But among you it will be different." Following Jesus always involves a reversal of thinking. He turns the world's values of power, approval, and status on their heads. We naturally want those things, but Jesus calls us to be radically different—to serve, to give, and to love, especially those we naturally overlook or despise.

> That's the point: "But among you it will be different."

How do we know if we're truly Jesus' disciples? By our sacrificial love for people outside our natural walls. They are, Jesus insists, our neighbors.

The Value You Add

Love often carries a cost—maybe not a big one, but at least a little one. The Samaritan gave time, attention, bandages, and money. For us, the price tag may not be as steep, but it can still be significant. Every act of kindness adds value to the recipient in three ways.

1. *We connect with the person's heart.*

    Not long ago, I was asked to speak at a church in another part of the country. When I arrived at the hotel, it was a little past my normal dinnertime. I asked the lady at the front desk for a recommendation for a restaurant. It didn't take a mind reader to realize she had lived a hard life. I didn't know the details, but her story was written in the lines on her face. When I asked for her advice about a place to eat, her face lit up. She told me about her favorite restaurant: "I go there every year for my birthday [which, she explained, wasn't for another six months]. It's a special place for me." I asked her to tell me about it, and she gave me every detail of what she orders—the same thing every year when her birthday rolls around. The dessert she always gets is the house-made cheesecake.

I went to the restaurant and followed her menu recommendations. Before I left, I ordered a piece of cheesecake. When I got back to the hotel, she was still on duty. I gave the cheesecake to her with a card that said, "I won't be here for your birthday, but I wanted to give you an early present. Happy birthday!"

She started to cry and asked, "Would it be okay if I come from behind the counter and give you a hug?"

I grinned. "Certainly."

For me, the cost of communicating value to this lady was six dollars for a piece of cheesecake, but this single act of love meant the world to her. The next morning as I was checking out, a man was at the reception counter. Before I left, I wrote the lady a note and asked him to give it to her. It said simply, "I believe in you and your future."

2. *We're free to love without any pressure.*

When we take a few minutes to add value to someone's life, we don't need to feel any pressure to pull out the Four Spiritual Laws, the Roman Road, or any other evangelistic tool. If we love people without any hidden agenda, we can begin to build a relationship of trust and affection. Someday—maybe soon and maybe not so soon—we'll probably have the opportunity to tell them how our faith in Jesus has had an impact on our lives.

3. *Spontaneity often signals authenticity.*

We don't need an elaborate program to demonstrate love. All of us can add value to people, and do it creatively, regularly, and lovingly. Write a note to your child's coach, give a small bouquet of flowers to a teacher, take time to introduce yourself to a person at church you don't know, visit someone who is homebound, wash a neighbor's car, let people go ahead of you in line, pay for the order of the person behind you in the drive-through, take time to thank every person who waits on you, take care of someone's children while they go to the doctor, give a larger tip than usual and engage the server, or buy a receptionist her favorite dessert. As you can tell, the list is endless. All it takes is a heart that wants to add value to the people we see each day.

Humility isn't thinking less of yourself; it's thinking of yourself less. Real humility isn't shame or self-hatred, and it doesn't make you less valuable. It gives you the heart and the power to value the people around you, especially those who aren't yet convinced they have any value at all.

Adding Value Gives Us a Voice

When we communicate value to people, they give us the privilege of having a voice in their lives—maybe for just a moment, but sometimes for a lifetime. Value gives us a voice in three ways:

1. *We speak into their past.*
   Many people are weighed down by past wounds or past failures, and they believe they are hopelessly flawed. Our words of comfort and understanding can begin (or continue) a healing process that can set them free.

2. *We speak into their present.*
   Everyone has questions, but few people have a wise, trusted mentor or friend who will take the time to listen and give them honest feedback. We can step into a person's life at a crucial juncture to provide the needed insight.

3. *We speak into their future.*
   People desperately need hope. No matter what they've done or where they've been, no matter how far they've fallen, God can weave all of that into a beautiful tapestry of anticipation for a far better future. Our description of a person's strengths and a vision for their tomorrow may be their first glimpse of something wonderful.

Jesus expanded the very definition of "neighbor." Are we listening?

THINK ABOUT IT

1. What do you think was going on in the law expert's mind when he asked, "Who is my neighbor?" and Jesus told him the story of the good Samaritan?

2. Describe the hero and the villains in the story. What are some reasons this story rocked the world of the religious leaders?

3. What are the walls between people in our culture? What are some reasons many of us feel justified in excluding "those people"?

4. Describe the differences between the world's values and Jesus' upside-down kingdom. What does it take to switch sides? What did it take for the disciples to do so?

5. Why do you think so many people are so deeply touched by simple acts of kindness?

PRAY ABOUT IT

Ask God to show you any walls between insiders and outsiders in your own heart. Focus on the fact that Jesus was the ultimate insider who came to suffer and die, paying the price to make us insiders in His kingdom. Thank Him for His grace.

DO IT

This week, add value to someone's life each day.
Right now, take a few minutes to think and pray
about these people and the ways you want to communicate love to them.

why is it so hard?

Graced people grace people. Healed people heal
people. Forgiven people forgive people. Loved
people love people. Accepted people accept people.

—Dino Rizzo

There may be any number of reasons why it's hard to love
someone. We've identified some of them: our schedules are
packed so we don't have time to stop and talk, we don't really
like the person, we don't trust them, we're creeped out by them,
or we feel pressured to tell them about Jesus even when they
haven't expressed any interest . . . to name just a few. I'm convinced that if we step into people's lives and genuinely meet
them where they are, many of them will want to know what's
different about us. Then it's easy to talk about Jesus.

I'm asked to speak at corporate meetings for some of the
largest companies in America. I've given more than a dozen
talks at the home offices of one of the telecom giants. Their
building is enormous—more like a city than an office. I was

the motivational speaker, with two thousand people in the auditorium and a simulcast to their offices across the country. For the six years I've been invited to speak there, I've had the opportunity to spend some time with the vice president of the company. Immediately after the last time I spoke there, an employee approached me and said, "Mr. Johnson wants to see you in his office."

"Now?" I asked.

"Yes, now." He turned and walked away. I was obviously expected to follow him.

On the way, my mind was racing. *Oh, gosh, what did I do? Did I say something that offended him? Is this my last rodeo with the company? How can I make this right?* Have you ever been there? Sure you have.

I walked into Mr. Johnson's office, and we began a pleasant conversation. After quite a while, my curiosity got the best of me. I asked, "Is there something you wanted to talk to me about? Was there a problem with my talk?"

He leaned forward and said, "Chris, you've been coming here for several years. You and I have had a number of brief conversations, but I've noticed . . . there's something different about you. You're not like anyone else who speaks at our gatherings." He paused for a few seconds and then asked, "What is it?"

I smiled. "Okay, but if I tell you, are we still going to be friends?"

He laughed. I took that as a positive sign, so I told him, "I think you may be seeing Jesus in me." We talked for a little while, and he was sincerely interested in what I had to say about finding forgiveness and purpose in Jesus. Since that day, we've talked several more times, and we've spent time together playing golf. He hasn't trusted in Jesus yet, but our relationship continues to grow. I didn't treat him like a target for evangelism, so there has been no pressure on him. He respects me and trusts me, so I don't feel any pressure either. That's the way it ought to be.

I used to speak at a lot of school events, and of course I couldn't talk about God in those messages. Each time, I asked God to use me to bring His light into the lives of the kids and their teachers. People often asked me, "Why in the world would you waste your time speaking in schools where you can't even mention God?"

I replied, "I don't believe it's a waste at all. Here's my perspective: you can legislate leaving His name unspoken, but you can't legislate leaving His presence unfelt."

Do people always ask about Jesus when we love them? No, but sometimes they do. And even when they don't, our acts of love and words of kindness break down barriers, so we can take the initiative when the time is right to tell them about Jesus.

When we see people as targets for evangelism, they know it and they don't like it one bit. But when we truly love people and God opens the door for us to talk about Jesus, they see us as friends who are simply sharing our hearts. We feel more comfortable, and they're far more likely to listen to our story of faith in Christ.

> Every relationship starts with love, is extended by love, and remains rooted in love no matter how the person responds.

See? It's not so hard after all. Every relationship starts with love, is extended by love, and remains rooted in love no matter how the person responds.

But there's another reason it's hard to love people who don't love us in return, and it's deeper—far deeper—than our words.

Missing God's Heart

I believe that the primary reason we find it hard to love others is that our own experience of God's love is anemic. Over the years I've observed a number of misguided approaches to God, especially these:

1. *We believe we must do enough.*

    We read passages in the Bible about love, and we sing in church about love, but if we peel back the layers of our hearts, many of us will find that we're still trying to measure up to earn God's approval. Earning isn't trusting. Decades ago, churches were criticized for being legalistic—that is, demanding that people follow rigid rules to be considered acceptable. In some corners of the country, the list of rules included "Don't drink," "Don't dance," "Don't cuss," "Don't go to movies where too much skin is showing—or any movies at all," and on the active side of the ledger, "Be in church every time the doors are open."

    Today, that's not really the problem. In many churches, the standards of performance to be "in good standing with God" have become more general, such as church attendance and giving. However, as with all measuring sticks of morality, how much is enough? If a person goes to church twice a month and gives twenty dollars each time, does that earn enough points with God? They never know.

2. *We believe we must be good enough.*

I'm sure we could find churches that still demand legalistic adherence to their rules, but we might have to look pretty hard. Instead, we find a softer form of performance-based acceptance: people don't have to obey religious rules, but they need to be "good enough" to be acceptable to God and others. Of course, being good enough is a sliding scale, depending on who defines the concept. Generally, though, it means we're reasonably pleasant, reasonably honest, and reasonably kind. "If we are," the concept promises, "God will surely accept us, He will reward us with success, and people will like us. After all, God grades on a curve, so doing pretty good is plenty good enough."

What's not to like? Actually, plenty. The belief that we need to be good enough is called "moralism." Don't get me wrong—I'm not against morals. It's a very good thing for our lives to be characterized by courage, honesty, generosity, and self-control, but it's a very different thing to trust in these as the basis of our salvation and acceptance by God!

In their book *Soul Searching*, sociologists Christian Smith and Melinda Lundquist Denton report on the study they conducted on the common beliefs of American teenagers (and later expanded to include their parents). Among their findings were these pervasive beliefs:

- God wants people to be good, nice, and fair to each other, as taught by the Bible and other world religions. (So far, so good. God certainly doesn't want us to be evil, mean, and unfair.)

- The central goal of life is to be happy and feel good
  about ourselves. (Well, no. Jesus was pretty clear that
  the central goal is to know Him, love Him, and follow Him wherever He leads.)
- Good people go to heaven when they die. (It seems
  like such a bland statement, but it captures the essence of what's off base about these beliefs. To the
  people surveyed, salvation—defined as going to
  heaven—is based on their performance instead of
  God's grace.)

The authors of the study concluded that people who
believe these things have missed God's grace![1] They
can't tap into the power of God's love because their
conception of His love is that it is a reward for being
good, not a gift in spite of them not being good.

To put it bluntly, we can't give away something we
don't possess. Or to put it another way, we can only
pour out the love that's in our emotional tanks. Trusting in our performance isn't close to grace; it's the
opposite of grace! It causes us to constantly measure
ourselves by other people, but comparison doesn't
produce love. If there's too little love in our emotional
tanks, we simply won't have the ability to love others.
We can try—and try like crazy—but sooner or later
we'll give up because it's just too hard.

3. *We believe we must give enough.*

For some of us, the measuring stick of being a good
enough person is generosity—not just of money but of
time and attention too. We read the Bible and see how
much God values a giving heart, and we conclude,

"That's it! I'll give everything I've got, and then God will approve of me and I'll feel good about myself!" The problem here is the motive. When we give to get something, we're not really giving at all—we're negotiating to get what we want.

These three misconceptions about how we relate to God seem totally reasonable because so many people believe them, and that's the way the world works, but they leave us empty, confused, and angry because we can never measure up. Many of us have a nagging sense of guilt. We may be haunted by a colossal past failure, a secret sin, or a ruined relationship, and the memories are still eating us alive. Old mistakes can seem far more real than God's present mercies, but we can't feel guilty enough for long enough to get rid of the feelings. So what's the answer?

The True Source

Many people have a hard time trusting in God. Why? Because you only trust the people you know, and for them God is only an abstract concept. Three passages in the Bible are crystal clear about the connection between our experience of God's love, forgiveness, and acceptance, and our ability to express it in our relationships:

1. *Love.* The first passage is one we've already seen. In his first letter, John tells us, "This is real love—not that we loved God, but that he loved us and sent his Son as a sacrifice to take away our sins. Dear friends, since God loved us that much, we surely ought to love each

other" (1 John 4:10–11). Jesus is our source of love—our love for Him and our love for others.

Many people secretly worry that they'll do something that will make God stop loving them. They don't yet grasp His grace: there's nothing they can do to lose God's love because there's nothing they did to earn it.

2. *Forgiveness.* When someone hurts you, what response does love require? Our instant and instinctive reaction is "fight, flight, or freeze," but there's a better way. This insight is found in Paul's letter to the Christians in Ephesus:

> Get rid of all bitterness, rage, anger, harsh words, and slander, as well as all types of evil behavior. Instead, be kind to each other, tenderhearted, forgiving one another, just as God through Christ has forgiven you.
>
> Imitate God, therefore, in everything you do, because you are his dear children. Live a life filled with love, following the example of Christ. He loved us and offered himself as a sacrifice for us, a pleasing aroma to God. (Eph. 4:31–5:2)

We can forgive others only to the extent we've experienced God's forgiveness in Christ. Then love can flow out of us like it flowed out of Jesus.

How long does it take to forgive, especially if the wound is deep? Forgiveness always involves the process of grief because we've suffered significant loss, and grieving takes time. We forgive as soon as we can and as deeply as we can.

Don't wait to start. You are responsible for how long what hurt you continues to haunt you.

3. *Acceptance.* The third passage is found near the end of Paul's letter to the believers in Rome. Earlier in this letter, he described the beauty and power of God's grace, and he explained that grace makes a difference in our relationships and choices. The church in Rome had both Jews and Gentiles as members, and they had a long history of tension. Paul didn't tell them, "Try hard not to hate each other!" Instead, he pointed to Jesus: "Therefore, accept each other just as Christ has accepted you so that God will be given glory" (Rom. 15:7).

We can only love the unlovely and accept people we might think are unacceptable if our hearts have been revolutionized by this truth: we were unacceptable because of our sin, but Jesus paid the price so we could belong to Him.

Don't Miss This!

What's the engine of genuine, compassionate, glad, sacrificial love? It's the power generated from our deepening grasp of God's love for us—that He has forgiven all our sins and accepts us in spite of our flaws . . . all because Jesus paid the price we couldn't pay. That's the gospel. Some people assume we believe the gospel when we become Christians and we don't ever need it again. I disagree. (And more importantly, Jesus, Paul, John, Peter, and every other writer in the Bible disagrees!) The gospel of grace is the starting point in our relationship with God, and it's the power that motivates us to live wholeheartedly for Jesus all day every day. We never get beyond the wonder of God's amazing grace poured out for us in Jesus. Paul explained that our growing appreciation for God's grace transforms our motives, our commitments, and our behavior:

> Christ's love controls us. Since we believe that Christ died for all, we also believe that we have all died to our old life. He died for everyone so that those who receive his new life will no longer live for themselves. Instead, they will live for Christ, who died and was raised for them. (2 Cor. 5:14–15)

The love of Jesus purifies our motives, energizes our passions, and empowers our plans. Left to ourselves, we give up or just go through the motions without the thrill of expecting God to do great things. We can obey God for the wrong reason of proving that we deserve His love, or we can obey because we're convinced we've already received it. When the love of God captures our hearts, our lives are characterized by "a long obedience in the same direction."[2] Jesus is more than enough, we're glad to belong to Him, and we want every moment of every day to count in His kingdom.

> When the love of God captures our hearts, our lives are characterized by "a long obedience in the same direction."

I'm afraid that we can regularly go to church, read the Bible, pray, and be in small groups . . . and completely miss the grace of God. Don't be surprised. It's happened before. The Pharisees were the most religious people on the planet. They did everything they thought God wanted them to do (and did it religiously), but they trusted in their goodness instead of God's grace to overcome their sins.

Theology professor Bryan Chapell has identified three common misunderstandings that poison our hearts. He calls them "the deadly be's." The first one is "be like." We hear messages and read Bible stories about Abraham, Moses, Daniel, David, and the rest, and we think, *I just need to be like them, then I'll be acceptable!*

The second misunderstanding is "be good." This is blatantly self-improvement and trusting in our performance, and this misconception of Christianity is rampant in our churches. The idea is that we can be good enough to win God's approval, and we can change our lives by trying really hard. Neither is true.

The third error is "be disciplined" in "being like" and "being good." In other words, "Whatever you're doing to make yourself more acceptable, do it even better!"[3]

Let me be clear: there's nothing wrong with following the example of a hero, trying to be good, or being more disciplined . . . unless we're trusting in these things to give us right standing with God. In that case, we've substituted ourselves as the agents of salvation instead of trusting in God's grace. The deadly be's always lead to one of two destinations: pride if we believe we're doing them better than someone else, or shame when we realize we've failed again. (And most of us vacillate between the two.)

It's a very human tendency to believe we have to prove ourselves. After all, that's how life works everywhere else! But it's deadly in the spiritual realm. Those who assume they're measuring up to God's standards are some of the most difficult people in the world to relate to. They think, feel, and act like they're superior to the rest of us. But those who aren't doing so well at the deadly be's feel like colossal failures. They often beat themselves up (by calling themselves names their mothers would be appalled at), and they try to feel bad enough for long enough to make up for their flaws. And as I mentioned, some of us are so creative that we can flip between self-righteousness and self-pity in a heartbeat.

The truth is that we had nothing to offer God to impress Him. Our performance fell far short of His requirements, so we deserved judgment. We were sunk! Things looked hopeless, but God's remedy was to send His Son. The Creator became a servant. The infinite became finite. The powerful became vulnerable. Why? Only because He loves us. Self-improvement alone never produces a tender heart and a wealth of love. In fact, it makes us more self-absorbed than ever! But when our hearts are melted by God's amazing grace, He can then mold them to be a little more like His—loving the unlovely, forgiving those who offend us, and accepting people who are very different from us.

How far did Jesus go to find us, love us, and bring us back? Sixteen centuries ago, Augustine captured the essence of Jesus when he wrote,

> Man's maker was made man that He, Ruler of the stars, might nurse at His mother's breast; that the Bread might hunger, the Fountain thirst, the Light sleep, the Way be tired on his journey; that the Truth might be accused of false witness, the Teacher be beaten with whips, the Foundation be suspended on wood; that Strength might grow weak; that the Healer might be wounded; that Life might die.[4]

Believe it. Bask in it. Think often about it, and you'll begin to love like Jesus loves.

Growing in Grace

As we grow in our experience of God's love, forgiveness, and acceptance, two things happen: we increasingly marvel that God would pay such a price to show His love to us, and we're more honest about the excuses we've used to avoid the risk and inconvenience of loving people.

At a meeting for university students sponsored by Veritas Forum, a Christian apologist spoke eloquently about the logic of faith in Christ. In the middle of his talk, he explained how a sense of wonder is essential to a vibrant, active faith, but very little amazes us anymore. As we grow up and become adults, it takes more "wow factor" to stun us. For example:

- A baby is amazed by a toy suspended above the crib.
- A toddler is amazed by the noise she can create by banging a pot with a spoon.
- A grade school child is amazed by the challenge of a new skill.
- A teenager is amazed by feats of daring and by sexual impulses.
- But an adult is seldom amazed at all.

We delight in those things that amaze us, not those that bore us. Our hearts thrill at the touch and sound of our firstborn, someone's love when we are in need, something awe-inspiring in nature, or God's answer to prayer. David was amazed at God's incredible beauty. He wrote,

> The one thing I ask of the LORD—
> the thing I seek most—

is to live in the house of the L<small>ORD</small> all the days of my
life,
delighting in the L<small>ORD</small>'s perfections
and meditating in his Temple. (Ps. 27:4)

I have to ask myself, *Is the Lord delightful to me? Are the depth of His love and His awesome power amazing to me?* If not, then my grasp of God has been eroded. My faith can only be as strong as my sense of wonder at the greatness and grace of God.

The level of our sense of wonder is a clear indicator of our grasp of God's true nature. Some of us are so focused on our own desires that we have reduced the King of the universe to a vending machine we go to when we want something. Are you looking for wonder and mystery when you put a dollar in a vending machine? No, you get angry when you don't get exactly what you want—immediately! Author and psychologist Larry Crabb observes that many of us think of God as "a specially attentive waiter."[5] When we get good service from him, we give him a nice tip of thanks. When we don't get what we want, we complain.

If the gospel doesn't amaze us, we really don't get it. The message is that the God of the universe stepped out of the splendor of heaven to sacrifice himself for you and me. Why in the world would Jesus do that? It's only because of love: "Amazing love, how can it be that Thou my God shouldst die for me?"[6]

As we become more secure in God's love, we can afford to be more objective about the excuses we've used for not going out of our way to love people:

- "I think I'm too busy to stop and get involved."
- "I really can't afford it."

- "It'll take too much time."
- "That person is just too hard to love."
- "She won't appreciate it anyway."
- "I'm an introvert. Loving people doesn't come naturally to me."
- "He'll figure it out on his own. He doesn't need me to tell him what to do."
- "I've tried to help people in the past, and it bombed. Fool me once, shame on you. Fool me twice, shame on me."

For some of us, the reasons we don't love seem not only reasonable but unchangeable. I have a friend who has wrestled for his entire life with the effects of growing up in a home where love wasn't expressed. His father was emotionally distant and an alcoholic. He told me there wasn't a single time in his childhood that his dad hugged him or told him he loved him. His mother was just the opposite: she smothered him with attention and directions. She thought it was love, but it communicated that he couldn't make decisions on his own.

After my friend got married, he replicated these relationships with his wife and kids. He became emotionally distant from his wife, but he was emotionally dominating with his two children, treating them like little kids when they were in junior high and high school. Finally, someone in his church asked him to have a cup of coffee, and he shared what he'd seen in my friend's life. It devastated him, but he knew it was true. Suddenly all the anger, all the fear, and all the shame he had internalized in his childhood made sense. And he resolved to do whatever it took to change.

The process was painful, but he learned to experience the love of God more deeply than ever, and gradually the way he treated his family was transformed. He and his wife now have a wonderful connection, and his children respect and like him.

He told me, "I don't know what would have happened if that guy hadn't spoken the truth to me. I never would have dreamed that my relationships with my wife and kids could be so great! No more isolation, no more possessive control, no more resentment, and no more shame."

> Love changes everything, but we don't just wake up one morning and love like Jesus.

We may be thinking of other excuses to add to the list, but they all melt away when the love of God becomes more real to us than our reasons for holding back. Love changes everything, but we don't just wake up one morning and love like Jesus. Here are some important steps:

1. The crucial first step is to admit, if it's true, that our sense of wonder at God and His creation isn't what it needs to be.
2. We need to accept His forgiveness and thank Him.
3. When we read the Scriptures, we ask God to open the eyes of our hearts to see what the Bible says about His strength and kindness.
4. As we pray, we take time to reflect on God's infinite wisdom, power, and compassion instead of rushing through a grocery list of requests. Like the psalmist, we reflect on God's greatness that can never be grasped, and we look for the work of God around us.

We can walk outside at night and gaze at the stars, hike in a national forest, or go to a natural history museum. When we read about a new scientific discovery, we can marvel at the incredible creativity of God and His willingness to let us take a peek at a sliver of His genius in creation. And as we consider Jesus' sacrifice for us, we can marvel that we were completely disqualified from His kingdom because of our sins, but Jesus qualified us by paying the ultimate price that we couldn't pay. And that amazes us.

Hoops

When we trust in our performance, we don't live a life of grace, peace, and love because we're so wrapped up in our pride and shame, and our message about Jesus gets terribly muddled. We make it hard for people in our communities to understand the message of grace. Instead, we expect them to jump through our hoops. In many churches the unspoken philosophy is, "Come to us and adopt our ways, and you'll be acceptable." If this strategy worked, churches would be bursting at the seams! But it doesn't. And they aren't. Churches continue to close in record numbers, and many more remain on life support. We need a different solution so we can break through the impasse and have a profound impact on our cities.

When we get outside ourselves, we can have an amazing influence. Individuals can get involved in organizations that are already making a difference. Small group leaders can mobilize their people to adopt a school, a fire station, or a police precinct, or partner with a nonprofit. Pastors can marshal their churches to have a powerful and positive presence, care for people in the community, and become a valuable resource to their city leaders. At that point, pastors don't just lead their churches; they earn the opportunity to lead their cities.

We sometimes think we need a title to have an impact. Certainly, having a title can open some doors, but Jesus modeled a different strategy. He didn't wear fancy robes or lobby to get into high positions. He just loved people. His impact was so powerful that He became a magnet, drawing people to himself, as well as a lightning rod of criticism because He didn't fit the mold of other religious leaders. When we step into the mess of our cities to love like that, we'll become a magnet and a lightning rod too. Our love will attract people to Jesus, but as always, no good deed goes unpunished. Somebody will ridicule us even when our motives are pure.

Hope and Help

In the earliest account of the church in Acts, Luke tells us that the believers got involved in the lives of people in Jerusalem and then in other communities throughout the Roman Empire. Believers weren't hidden away in their own subculture; they were engaged, involved, and integrated into the life of the community.

It's a well-known fact that the population of Christians in the Roman Empire exploded from about 6 percent to about 50 percent in only two hundred years.[7] How did this happen? There are many factors: the Christian faith valued women more than pagan religions did; Christians didn't expose children to the elements and leave them to die because they didn't want them, so more children in these families became believers; and improvements in communication and travel throughout the empire facilitated the spread of the gospel. Perhaps the most fascinating reason for the rapid rise of Christianity is found in the impact of two catastrophic plagues. In AD 165 and again in AD 260, about a fourth of the people in the Roman Empire died, probably first from smallpox and secondly from measles.

In his book *The Rise of Christianity*, sociologist Rodney Stark describes the impact of these events. When the plagues struck, pagans (including doctors) fled the cities to save their own lives, leaving the sick to manage on their own. Of course, unattended victims of serious diseases have a very high mortality rate. But in this tragedy, the Christians stepped up and stepped in. The pagans had no hope of an afterlife, so saving their own skins was of ultimate importance. The Christians had a strong belief in heaven and the ultimate resurrection, so they had more courage to face disease and impending death. Their care for the sick had a profound effect. We can see the difference in the response from writings of that day. The historian Thucydides described the futility of the pagan doctors and priests:

> The doctors were quite incapable of treating the disease because of their ignorance of the right methods. . . . Equally useless were prayers made in the temples, consultation of the oracles, and so forth; indeed, in the end people were so overcome by their sufferings that they paid no further attention to such things.[8]

Family members of unbelievers weren't any more helpful. Dionysius, a church leader, explained their panicked response:

> The heathen behaved in the very opposite way [from the Christians]. At the first onset of the disease, they pushed the

sufferers away and fled from their dearest, throwing them into the roads before they were dead and treated unburied corpses like dirt, hoping thereby to avert the spread and contagion of the fatal disease; but do what they might, they found it difficult to escape.[9]

The Christians weren't immune from the dangers of the plagues, but their faith gave them courage to stay in the cities, to nurse their own sick, and to care for the pagans who had been abandoned by their families. Dionysius described their faith, courage, and love:

> Most of our brother Christians showed unbounded love and loyalty, never sparing themselves and thinking only of one another. Heedless of danger, they took charge of the sick, attending to their every need and ministering to them in Christ, and with them departed this life serenely happy; for they were infected by others with the disease, drawing on themselves the sickness of their neighbors and cheerfully accepting their pains. Many, in nursing and curing others, transferred their death to themselves and died in their stead. . . . The best of our brothers lost their lives in this manner, a number of [leaders] and laymen, winning high commendation so that death in this form, the result of great piety and strong faith, seems in every way the equal of martyrdom.[10]

Does this kind of love for those in need seem logical to you because you believe God is good, and no matter what happens now, the end will always be a glorious resurrection in the presence of Jesus? Or does the risk of death by caring for strangers seem crazy to you? Hope gives us the power to help. When disaster struck, Christians in the second and third centuries stepped up and stepped in to meet glaring needs.

Let me ask you: what are you doing as people are dying—emotionally, spiritually, and relationally, if not physically—all around you?

Imagine an atheist driving in front of your church. They might think, *What wasted property! That land could be used for something productive, like apartments or an office building.* Or, when they look at your church and consider the impact you're having on the community, they might draw a differ-ent conclusion: *I don't follow their beliefs or practice their faith, but I shudder at the thought of what would happen to our city if they weren't here. Those people love firefighters, police officers, the mentally challenged, the physically disabled, divorced moms, unwed mothers, the elderly, and lots of other groups in our city. The mayor depends on the pastor. Other churches may not make much of a dent in our community, but this one sure does!*

> What are you doing as people are dying—emotionally, spiritually, and relationally, if not physically—all around you?

That was the impact of the Christians in the Roman Empire in the first centuries after Christ, and it can be the impact of our churches today . . . but only when we drink deeply of the grace of God, the love of God, and the power of God.

What are you drinking?

THINK ABOUT IT

1. Why is moralism—trying to be a good enough person to be accepted by God and people—counterproductive, and how does it keep us from really loving people?

2. What is the connection between wonder and our ability to love others?

3. What excuses (or "good reasons") have you used to guard your heart and protect your privacy so you can avoid the messiness of getting involved in the lives of hurting people? Why do you think these excuses feel so right?

4. Reflect on the compassion and courage of the Christians who cared for plague victims. How does certainty about our ultimate hope give us courage to get involved with people today?

5. If an atheist drove by your church today, what conclusions would they draw about its impact on your city based on its reputation?

PRAY ABOUT IT

Ask God to reveal any inclination in your heart to prove yourself acceptable to Him by your behavior. Thank Him for the wonder of His forgiveness and grace. Ask Him to remind you that your hope isn't in this life, so you have nothing to lose by giving yourself wholeheartedly to care for others.

DO IT

This action step is personal examination. Self-analysis is hard work, but that's exactly what I'm asking of you. How much are you drinking of moralism, and how much are you drinking of God's grace, love, wisdom, and power? What would it take for God's love to become so real to you that it overflows into the lives of the people around you? Is that something you want? Explain your answer.

the call

When we are in touch with God's joy and peace
in us, then we become whole and holy persons.
Like living torches, we radiate the light and heat
of God's compassionate love.

—Mark Yaconelli

A couple—I'll call them James and Barbara—who owns their
own business live in a condo complex. One afternoon when
they were at home, they noticed a lot of kids hanging around
after school. They realized these kids needed some attention,
so they took the initiative to create an after-school program
every Wednesday. They let parents know they were going to
host children with games, arts and crafts, and snacks. The first
week, two kids came. The second week, five came. After six
weeks, any skepticism on the part of the parents had vanished,
and fifteen eager kids showed up.

Owning and running a business is more than a full-time
job, but James and Barbara closed their shop every Wednesday

afternoon to care for these kids. The love they shared with them had an impact. About ten children soon started attending the couple's church, and five sets of parents soon followed.

During this time, James and Barbara didn't ask the church for any resources. In fact, they didn't even tell church leaders what they were doing.

Four months after they started the program, the couple drove up to their church with a van full of kids. Their surprised pastor asked them who the kids were, and James explained, "Oh, they're part of our Wednesday thing."

"What Wednesday thing?"

"The after-school program."

The pastor had no idea they were caring for these children. He asked the couple to tell him about it, and Barbara said, "We saw a need, and we sensed God's leading to meet it. It's no big deal, really, but we have more joy than ever before."

James chimed in, "We were made for this!"

James and Barbara's decision to get involved with kids moved them from success to significance. Their sense of God's call to serve kids propelled them beyond the money they would have made if they had invested those hours every Wednesday in their business; beyond any need for recognition, because the only people they told were the parents of the kids; and beyond any status or title, because they served with humility. To them, it was time well spent. They were serving God with integrity in their business—that's part of God's call—but seeing the kids tugged at their hearts. As James pointed out, they had found the thing God had created them to do.

Call and Purpose

When people hear the word "call" or that someone feels "called by God," many immediately assume the speaker is talking about full-time Christian service. That definition is much too narrow. No one becomes a Christian without first hearing and following God's call to trust in Jesus. At that moment, everything in them is reoriented around Jesus. In his book *The Call*, Os Guinness defines our spiritual calling as "the truth that God calls us to himself so decisively that everything we are, everything we do, and everything we have is invested with a special devotion and dynamism lived out as a response to his summons and service."[1] This invitation isn't only for super Christians or professional Christians—it's true of all believers.

We get a clear picture of God's call in the story of Abraham, a man who lived about four thousand years ago but whose life is completely relevant today. The first eleven chapters of Genesis tell us that human history was spiraling downward and God's purposes looked like a distant dream. Into the mess, God spoke to Abraham, who lived in Ur, a community in what is now Iraq. God told him,

> Leave your native country, your relatives, and your father's family, and go to the land that I will show you. I will make you into a great nation. I will bless you and make you famous, and you will be a blessing to others. I will bless those who bless you and curse those who treat you with contempt. All the families on earth will be blessed through you. (Gen. 12:1–3)

Concepts about the Call

1. *The call is open-ended.*

God's call was significant for what it wasn't as well

as for what it was. He didn't tell Abraham, "I'm sending you to this particular place to do this particular thing." He just told him to leave home with his family and trust Him for directions along the way. Imagine packing your family in the SUV and telling them, "We're moving to another city, but I don't know where we're going. God will show us. Don't worry. No, no one has ever done this before, but I'm sure it'll work out!"

The call of God is open-ended. We step out without any guarantees of where He will lead us. That's the risk—and the adventure.

2. *The call is based in the relationship, not the role.*

The most important feature of God's call in our lives isn't about a task He wants us to do; it's about trusting Him to love us and lead us. God's direction to play a particular role or accomplish a specific task comes out of this relationship.

3. *The call doesn't have a straight line to its fulfillment.*

God gave Abraham some very specific promises: the first one was that he and his wife, Sarah, would become "a great nation." It sounds wonderful, but it was completely unreasonable. At that point Abraham was seventy-five years old and Sarah was sixty-five—somewhat past the time when they should be thinking about buying a crib and painting the spare bedroom for a nursery. How in the world would God pull that off? They had no clue! In fact, God would make them wait another twenty-five years before He fulfilled this promise. Inevitable delays are part of God's call.

4. *The call inspires generosity.*

Another part of the promise is that God would bless Abraham so that he could be a blessing to others. God's generous provisions of talents, health, money, time, freedom, and opportunities are never an end in themselves. They aren't for us; they're for others. We're channels of blessing, and God calls us to use everything entrusted to us to enable others to thrive. Jesus came to give, serve, and bless, and as we follow Him, we give to, serve, and bless the people around us.

The work of God—in salvation, in spiritual growth, in caring for those in need, and in changing the culture of a community—always involves financial sacrifice. For each of us, the statement is true: someone somewhere gave something to get us here. God's call always prompts us to invest our resources in the lives of others.

Abraham and Sarah didn't exactly experience a smooth, straight-line path to the fulfillment of God's call. They had many ups and downs, successes and failures, joys and heartaches. Through it all, God broke through to encourage them when they were discouraged and remind them that He is faithful—no matter how bleak things looked at the moment.

The call of God rests on His faithfulness, His power, and His timing. This means we need an expansive grasp of God's character so our faith doesn't fail in tough times. Guinness reminds us, "God calls people to himself, but this call is no casual suggestion. He is so awe inspiring and his summons so commanding that only one response is appropriate—a response as total and universal as the authority of the Caller."[2]

God created each of us for a purpose. His call is His initiative to show us who He is, who we are, and what He wants us to do. The call isn't our idea; it's God's. We don't stumble into our purpose; God awakens us to it.

No Limits

Abraham didn't put any limits on God's call. He didn't demand clarity, guarantees, or comfort. He just said, "Yes, Lord. Let's go." I'm sure he had a thousand questions along the way, and later in the story we find him reasoning with God. There's nothing wrong with that, because Abraham was committed to following God with all his heart—wherever He led, however long it took to get there, and whatever struggles were part of the journey.

Many of us try to put restrictions on God's call. We may not use these exact words, but our attitude is, "Lord, I'll follow You *as long as* You make it easy for me"; "I'll follow You, but *only if* You'll give me the lover I want, the money I desire, and the lifestyle I prefer"; or "I'll follow You, *but only when* You share the spotlight with me."

> Here's the truth: we are called to be colaborers with Christ, not costars.

Here's the truth: we are called to be colaborers with Christ, not costars. As we've seen, some people are convinced they've done enough for God and have given enough to God, so they've discharged their obligations. They wouldn't say it out loud, but in their hearts they believe God owes them. They don't really get it. God's call is always based on His authority and character, and it's always first to love, honor, and serve Him. Only then is it about the way He wants us to serve Him.

Paul captured the source of the call and our right response in his letter to the Romans. After eleven chapters of describing the way God has rescued us from sin, death, and hell by His grace, he encourages us:

And so, dear brothers and sisters, I plead with you to give your bodies to God because of all he has done for you. Let them be a living and holy sacrifice—the kind he will find acceptable. This is truly the way to worship him. Don't copy the behavior and customs of this world, but let God transform you into a new person by changing the way you think. Then you will learn to know God's will for you, which is good and pleasing and perfect. (Rom. 12:1–2)

The only reasonable response to God is, "Lord, You created me, so I'm Yours. You bought me, so I'm Yours. You adopted me, so I'm Yours. Whatever You want me to do, I'll do. Wherever You want me to go, I'll go. Whoever You want me to love, I'll love."

Does that scare you or thrill you? Both? Yeah, me too.

Treasure

Being a Christian is more than ticking the boxes on the checklist of minimum requirements to belong to a church. That's another form of moralism, not real faith in the real God. In fact, following Jesus begins not with what *we have to do* but with what *God has already done* for us.

The Bible has some magnificent passages about our identity as God's people. A favorite of mine is in Peter's first letter. After describing people who have rejected Christ, Peter draws a contrast: "But you are not like that, for you are a chosen people. You are royal priests, a holy nation, God's very own possession. As a result, you can show others the goodness of God, for he called you out of the darkness into his wonderful light" (1 Pet. 2:9). Jewish readers in the first century (and today) would instantly recognize that this language comes from Exodus 19–20, one of the most famous passages in the Old Testament, when God gave Moses the Ten Commandments.

We are "a chosen people." This means God has taken the initiative to rescue us and make us His own. We are "royal priests," which is an astounding blend of the two most important roles in God's kingdom. We are "a holy nation," not by our own performance but because Christ's righteous life has been credited to us. And we are "God's very own possession," a term that means "treasure." Get this: God values us so much that He considers us His treasure, worth more than the stars in the sky and all the diamonds and gold found in the earth!

The problem, of course, is that most of us simply don't believe it. Our thinking, our self-assessment, doesn't come close to what God says about us. If we get a glimpse of the wonder of God's grace, we'll be humbled by the fact that He loves us in spite of all our flaws, and we'll be thrilled that He considers us His beloved children.

Identity is always imparted by someone else. We've gotten our sense of self largely from our relationships with our parents. For some of us, the love and security we experienced made it easy to believe God adores us. But many of us, to one degree or another, had less than stellar home environments. For us, grasping the depth and width and length of God's love is harder, but it's perhaps even sweeter because of the contrast with what we've experienced in the past.

Amazingly, the love of God for you and me—not merely an academic concept but His tender, strong affection—is limitless. Jesus said that He loves us as much as the Father loves Him (John 15:9), and the Father loves us as much as He loves Jesus (John 17:23). It doesn't get any better than that!

Voices

All of us have internalized messages about who we are—our identity, the foundation of our security and value. For decades, as I've talked with people, I've noticed that a relative handful of people have a very strong, biblical sense of identity. Those who do, experience the twin characteristics of peace and drive—at the same time. They aren't terrified of failure or rejection, so they can channel their energies into activities that make a difference. But many of us are plagued by voices that condemn, belittle, and shame us. They may come from our childhood, our own misplaced desires and fears, or the enemy of our souls—or more likely, a combination of these sources. What do they sound like? Here are some common messages many of us hear in the depths of our hearts:

"I can't afford to fail."

"I can't afford to be wrong, or I'll look foolish."

"I have to exceed others' expectations to feel good about myself."

"I can't let people know what's really going on with me, or they'll leave me or make fun of me."

"I have to always be on guard to protect myself."

"I'm worthless, flawed, and unlovable."

"I'm plagued by comparison: not as smart as . . . , not as handsome as . . . , not as gifted as . . ."

"The only way to feel good about myself is to sacrifice myself for others. I keep giving, but I never feel okay."

God's call shouts a very different set of messages! First He tells us who we are, and then He tells us how to express our new identity. We can remind ourselves that instead of those condemning statements, we can hear:

"Because of Christ, I'm loved, forgiven, and accepted by God."

"I'll never be more loved than I am right now through Christ. The Father loves me as much as He loves Jesus."

"When God adopted me (Rom. 8:15–17), I was instantly and completely in Christ. The Father delights in me as much as He delights in Jesus, not because my performance has impressed Him but because the sacrifice of Christ impresses Him."

"Christ took the punishment I deserved so that I could receive the love, honor, and acceptance He deserves."

"God will never leave me nor forsake me."

"God has given me a future and a hope."

And because we're secure in God's love, we can:

Serve gladly.

Forgive those who have hurt us.

Move toward those who are different from us.

Care for people who don't care for us.

Restructure our priorities to reflect God's values.
Live for Jesus and the people Jesus loves . . . which is
   everybody!

The call of God changed Abraham's identity, direction, and
actions. After God spoke to him, he was never the same. The
call has the same impact on us. As we increasingly internalize
God's voice, the love of Jesus will be so real to us that we can't
contain it. That's what it means to love like Jesus loves.

Overflow

This is who we are in Christ—loved, forgiven, accepted,
adopted, and treasured. How can we let these truths sink in
so they become the dominant way we think about God and
about ourselves? By focusing on Jesus. He took advantage of
built-in events in the culture and calendar to show people who
He was. The feasts of the Jewish people were very important to
them, and Jesus often went to Jerusalem to participate. One of
them, the Feast of Tabernacles, celebrated the annual harvest.
The feast was eight days long, full of ceremonial washings and
sacrifices, all building up to a crescendo on the last day. The
temple grounds were packed with people. John tells us what
happened:

> On the last day, the climax of the festival, Jesus stood and
> shouted to the crowds, "Anyone who is thirsty may come to
> me! Anyone who believes in me may come and drink! For the
> Scriptures declare, 'Rivers of living water will flow from his
> heart.'" (When he said "living water," he was speaking of the
> Spirit, who would be given to everyone believing in him. But

the Spirit had not yet been given, because Jesus had not yet entered into his glory.) (John 7:37–39)

I believe every person has a God-given thirst that can only be quenched by a relationship with the God of love. Sadly, most people go to the wrong fountains: success, pleasure, prestige, comfort, and power, to name a few. When we drink of Christ, "rivers of living water" flow from our hearts. What does that look like? It's gratitude, joy, compassion, and active service for others. The life of Jesus flows into us and overflows out of us. But this kind of spiritual life can't be manufactured; it's the result of the Holy Spirit working God's love deep into the recesses of our hearts, so it permeates everything we are, everything we do, and everything we say.

> How can we let these truths sink in so they become the dominant way we think about God and about ourselves? By focusing on Jesus.

As Paul looked back near the end of his life, he was reassured that his life counted. He had answered God's call, and God had done remarkable things through him. In the last chapter of his last letter, Paul wrote Timothy: "As for me, my life has already been poured out as an offering to God. The time of my death is near. I have fought the good fight, I have finished the race, and I have remained faithful. And now the prize awaits me—the crown of righteousness, which the Lord, the righteous Judge, will give me on the day of his return" (2 Tim. 4:6–8). Paul had answered the call. He had surrendered his life to Jesus on the road to Damascus decades before, and he had followed Jesus wherever He led him.

Paul called himself a bondservant. That term had a very specific meaning. Many slaves were actually indentured servants working off a debt, and when it was paid by their years of service, they were free to go. However, if the servant loved his master and wanted to stay, the master used an awl to pierce the servant's ear as a sign to everyone that he had chosen to remain with his master (Deut. 15:17). That's our condition too. We've been set free by the payment of Christ on the cross, but if we realize how much the Master loves us, we'll choose to remain under His care and gladly continue to serve Him.

Years ago, I heard a pastor say that he wanted to "die empty." He didn't mean abandoned and forsaken; he meant that he wanted to leave it all on the field—to spend every ounce of energy, time, and resources to make Christ known. But we don't have to wait until we're seventy to have this perspective. We can have it when we're seventeen. No matter where we've come from, how many mistakes we've made, or how old we are, if our hearts are beating, God isn't finished with us. When He is finished with us, we'll be dead. Until then, let's keep trusting, keep surrendering, keep serving, and keep loving.

> No matter where we've come from, how many mistakes we've made, or how old we are, if our hearts are beating, God isn't finished with us.

The call of God is to take everything He puts in our hands and use it to honor Him and make a difference in the lives of others. We're blessed to be a blessing. Jesus said, "When someone has been given much, much will be required in return" (Luke 12:48).

What has God given to you? How are you using all of it to bless others? We're called by God to love where we live. Believe it. Pour your energies into it. Live it.

THINK ABOUT IT

1. When you hear the term "called by God," do you instantly assume it refers to professional Christians? Explain your answer. Describe the elements of God's call in the life of every believer.

2. What lessons about God's call do you learn from the life of Abraham? Which of these is most meaningful to you?

3. On a scale of 0 (impossible) to 10 (got it—no problem), how difficult is it for you to believe you are God's treasure? Explain your answer. What messages—negative and positive—have you internalized? What can you do to have God's messages dominate your thoughts, your identity, and your actions?

4. What difference does it make to realize God has called us first *to be* (that is, to be His beloved children) and then, out of that security, *to do* (to give ourselves for the sake of others)? What happens when we get the order wrong and focus primarily on doing things for God?

5. What role does the Holy Spirit play in our understanding of God's call and our ability to live it out?

PRAY ABOUT IT

Look back through the chapter and mark passages of Scripture and statements that touch your heart. Take time to pray over these, and thank God for His amazing love.

DO IT

Make a list of the ways God has blessed you. (Don't stop with money!) Give yourself a score (0 is terrible, 10 is terrific) of how well you're using each one to honor God and bless others. Pick two and write a plan to use them more effectively as blessings for other people.

start small . . . but start!

You can always give without loving, but you can never love without giving.

—Amy Carmichael

During a Love Where You Live outreach sponsored by our church, a group of college students asked themselves, "What can we do that will make a difference?" Probably inspired by Blake Mycoskie, the founder of TOMS Shoes, they thought of going barefoot on campus for a few days to raise awareness of all the people in the world who don't have shoes. I found out about their idea and asked them to share their vision on a Sunday morning. Not surprisingly, people in our church were enthusiastic and gave generously to fund the effort to buy and ship shoes overseas. The college also promoted their plan and contributed to the cause. A local television station heard about these students and featured them on a segment of the news. Through donations of money and pairs of shoes, the students gathered enough to fill several garages. With the additional funds donated for shipping, they were able to put shoes on the feet of thousands of people in a remote corner of the globe. It all started with a simple conversation when one of the students asked the others, "What can we do to help?"

As a part of a church's Love Where You Live effort, a person in a small group felt touched by the statistics about foster kids in the area. She shared her concern with the group, and they instantly got on board. They wanted to do something that would bring joy to kids, and they decided new bicycles would be a great idea. But bikes cost money. They realized they could pool money from people in the group and buy a few bikes, but they wanted to do more. They held garage sales over four weekends and raised $5,000. After some bargaining with a store manager, they were able to buy fifty bikes. By coordinating with the local foster program to give the bikes away, they were able to make a lot of kids feel special. Again, it started with one person having a heart for kids who often feel lonely.

"You Feed Them"

One of the most famous of Jesus' miracles was the surprise dinner He threw for an intimate gathering of about twenty thousand. (There were five thousand men, so we can assume family members expanded the number quite considerably.) It's important to understand the background of the event. Jesus had been teaching crowds in Palestine, and He decided to spend some time in His hometown of Nazareth. When He taught there, people asked, "Who does He think He is? He's not that big a deal!"

Jesus left there, and soon He heard the terrible news that His cousin, John the Baptist, had been executed by the Jewish king, who was colluding with the Romans. Heartbroken, Jesus took a boat across the Sea of Galilee to a remote area. Although the people of Nazareth didn't respect Him, the rest of the people in that part of the country were amazed at His teaching and His power to heal, so thousands of them followed Him on foot. We pick up the story as Matthew describes it:

> That evening the disciples came to him and said, "This is a remote place, and it's already getting late. Send the crowds away so they can go to the villages and buy food for themselves."
> But Jesus said, "That isn't necessary—you feed them." (Matt. 14:15–16)

The disciples recognized the need. Twenty thousand people had traveled away from their homes and towns, where there was plenty of food, to a place in the middle of nowhere that didn't even have a Chick-fil-A—because you know it wouldn't be a Christian event without one! Their solution was for Jesus to send the people home so they could find something to eat before they fainted. Jesus had a different idea. He looked at the disciples and said, "You feed them."

Imagine being one of those guys. They were looking at a crowd that would have filled a large part of a football stadium, and Jesus told them to feed all the people. They must have been confused and exasperated when they responded, "But we have only five loaves of bread and two fish!" (v. 17). Other Gospel writers tell us that the disciples had commandeered a little boy who had brought his sack lunch. That was the only food on hand.

Jesus must have smiled when he told them, "Bring them here" (v. 18). Matthew tells us what happened next:

> Then he told the people to sit down on the grass. Jesus took the five loaves and two fish, looked up toward heaven, and blessed them. Then, breaking the loaves into pieces, he gave the bread to the disciples, who distributed it to the people. They all ate as much as they wanted, and afterward, the disciples picked up twelve baskets of leftovers. About 5,000 men were fed that day, in addition to all the women and children! (vv. 19–21)

Could Jesus have picked up rocks and turned them into bread? Yes. Could he have turned sticks into fish? Of course. Why did Jesus involve the disciples and the little boy? Because He wanted them to participate in the miracle. They couldn't do what He could do, but they could play a part. They didn't have much, but Jesus was glad to use what they had. The boy gave his lunch to the disciples and watched as Jesus turned it into a feast for thousands. The disciples offered Jesus all they had (and it wasn't even theirs!), and they became banquet servers to make sure everyone got plenty of bread and fish. After dinner, the disciples picked up the leftovers—twelve baskets full. Why twelve and not ten or eleven? Because all of the disciples were part of the process. No one was left out— not even Thomas, who probably doubted any of this would work out, and not even Judas, who Jesus knew was going to betray Him one day. This was an important lesson: the disciples learned that their small part could result in huge blessings for a lot of people. But my thoughts always drift back to the little boy. Just imagine the story he told the next morning at school!

In the Bible and in our lives, we see a clear principle: miracles follow action. It's not our power that performs miracles, but time after time, God waits for us to respond to His command, "You feed them," which is the trigger that propels His miraculous intervention. He healed a woman who had been bleeding for twelve years when she reached through the legs of people in the crowd to touch the hem of His robe as He walked by. Four guys cut a hole in a roof and dropped their friend in front of Jesus because the room was so crowded they couldn't get in the door, and Jesus healed their friend. He turned water into wine after He told the servants at a wedding to fill the huge stone containers, and they did it. In the same way, He wants us to participate in His work to change lives, provide resources, and restore hope. We only need to play a small role, but it's a crucial one. God doesn't give us the chair; He gives us the wood and the skill we need to make it.

> God doesn't give us the chair; He gives us the wood and the skill we need to make it.

The hard truth is that most of us will never see a miracle because we'll never do anything that requires one. In other words, we don't do our small part. Oh, we see the needs, and we complain about all the problems in our communities, but when Jesus says, "Do your part," we'd rather keep complaining than take action.

Close to Home

Love Where You Live begins in the family of God. On the night Jesus was betrayed, He spent time with the disciples before He was arrested. When I read John's account of that night, I'm struck by how many times He tells them, "Love one another." He began earlier in the evening when He gave them a "new commandment" to love each other as He had loved them, and He said that their relationships would be one of the brightest beacons of hope for people who were watching: "Your love for one another will prove to the world that you are my disciples" (John 13:35). He repeats this crucial command twice a couple of chapters later. Did John need an editor? Did Jesus forget what He'd said? No, love is how the family of God should relate to each other. And based on all of His repetitions, it must be pretty important to Jesus.

We won't have much of an impact on those outside the church if, when they look inside, they see people who can't get along with each other. They might call us hypocrites—and they might be right! *Yeah,* some of you are thinking, *that's easy for you to say. You don't know Sam [or Beth or Maria or Juan or William or whoever you don't like].* Yes, I know there are plenty of people in the church who are hard to love, but if people who have been rescued from hell by the grace of God can't express that love to each other, I'm afraid we won't express it to anyone.

> We won't have much of an impact on those outside the church if, when they look inside, they see people who can't get along with each other. They might call us hypocrites—and they might be right!

I'm certainly not suggesting that if people are believers there will be complete joy and happiness in all our relationships. The Bible is much too realistic for that. For instance, Paul's letters to the Corinthians address the systemic conflict among them caused by comparison and competition. His solution was for them to dive deeper into God's grace to find the strength to love each other. And his letter to the church in Philippi specifically calls out two women who were at each other's throats. (How would you like being featured in the Bible for being hard to get along with?)

If people are hard to love, instead of writing them off, a better angle is to assume they have some unrelieved pain from the past that's making them difficult today. (Of course, some people are genuinely unsafe. We need to be very careful if we're in relationships with abusers and people with personality disorders. Loving them means blocking, or at least limiting, their ability to harm us or others.) Look beyond the surface scowls and love them anyway. And remember, Jesus loved us when we were rebels and didn't care about Him. He didn't just shake His head and walk away. He entered our world to show us how much He loved us. If He was willing to die for you and me, maybe we can be willing to move toward someone we don't particularly like so we can speak words of kindness.

People put on their happy faces when they show up at church, but most of the people I know have some hurts and worries that are inwardly weighing them down. The people sitting to the right and left of you may not be as put together as they seem. They need a smile and a greeting, but they may also need someone to take care of their kids when they're going to see a lawyer because their marriage is dissolving; a meal because a family member is in the hospital; a babysitter because they haven't had a date in six months; a referral to a financial counselor because they're drowning in debt; or a shoulder to cry on because their teenager is pregnant, is doing drugs, or has run away. Not all problems are dramatic (thank God!), but we will never know how to love well until we listen, take the time to get beneath the surface, and give love more than lip service.

People who are drowning in hurt, fear, anger, and shame often assume their lives will never be any better. (Some of us have been there, and some of us are there now.) It's like they're living in the middle of a hurricane of pain and problems. One of the ways we can provide hope is to assure them that, eventually, every storm runs out of rain.

Paul uses the metaphor of the human body to illustrate the intricacy and importance of every part of the body of Christ, the church. The body functions amazingly well when it's healthy, but a disease or a wound left untreated can cause tremendous harm. Jesus' repeated directive to love each other means that it's essential for us to care for and avoid hurting each other. That means we don't post offensive messages and pictures about each other on social media. Love Where You Live starts with our spiritual family—and the people who live under our roofs. We look for ways to encourage and support each other; we're not reactive when people disagree; and when there are offenses, we resolve them by talking, forgiving, and healing. None of this can happen unless we treat each other as family members (or maybe better than we've treated some of the people in our families). Engage, don't be passive, and don't be snarky. People have rough edges, and how we respond when we feel rubbed shows what's really inside us. We can be sure of this: people outside the church are watching.

It's sobering to ask the hard questions: Do people in our communities find us attractive? Do they see a qualitative difference in how we treat each other? Are they amazed that we care so much about each other—and them? Is there any difference in our level of peace or worry from that of the rest of the community? Are our marriages stronger? Are our families happier? Are we more honest in business? Do we argue about politics with less venom than others?

> It's sobering to ask the hard questions: Do people in our communities find us attractive? Do they see a qualitative difference in how we treat each other?

Would other people say, "Wow, those people have huge hearts! They obviously love people who are really different from them. They actually listen before they give their opinions. They spend their time and resources to help others instead of buying the next gadget for themselves." If that's not what they say, then we're not fulfilling Jesus' command as much as we can or as much as He wants us to. When we're in a room with unbelievers, do we shine with the love of God so that people want to be near us, or are we obnoxious about our beliefs about faith, politics, sports, and everything else? Do our words and our behavior make people thirsty for Jesus or nauseated? Just asking.

Love the City

In the Information Age, anybody with an internet connection can speak out on anything and everything. Christians have taken advantage of the opportunity to voice their opinions, beliefs, and convictions on every conceivable topic. If we step back and consider those perspectives, we notice they come from different angles:

- Some believe that the culture is a reflection of Christ's kingdom values. They uncritically accept the trends in the culture and see no problem in accommodating different lifestyles and religions. They just want everyone to get along.
- Some see Christ and the culture in fierce opposition. This group is the most vocal and often the angriest. They believe the liberals (the people in the first group) are taking their rights away, and they're fighting back. Or they believe the conservatives are selfish brutes, and they're fighting back just as hard.
- Some believe Christ wants to use us to love people so much that culture is transformed. This group sees the tension between the values of Christ's kingdom and the unbelieving culture, but they are more compassionate than angry and more active than reactive.[1] (I'm sure you can tell where I'm going.)

Does the Bible say anything about how we should engage our culture? As a matter of fact, it does. In the prophet Jeremiah's time, Israel had been overrun by the Assyrians, and Judah had been devastated by the Babylonians. The temple had been destroyed, and many of the people had been marched into exile in Babylon. They were, to say the least, deeply discouraged. They hoped to hear from God that He would rescue them and restore the nation—and do it quickly! Instead, this is the message God gave them:

This is what the LORD of Heaven's Armies, the God of Israel, says to all the captives he has exiled to Babylon from Jerusalem: "Build homes, and plan to stay. Plant gardens, and eat the food they produce. Marry and have children. Then find spouses for them so that you may have many grandchildren. Multiply! Do not dwindle away! And work for the peace and prosperity of the city where I sent you into exile. Pray to the LORD for it, for its welfare will determine your welfare." (Jer. 29:4–7)

The people wanted to play the victim card, but God wouldn't let them. They wanted a quick out, but God told them to stay there and "work for the peace and prosperity of the city." He wasn't talking about Jerusalem. He was talking about Babylon, the nation that had destroyed all they held dear and was holding them captive! God told them, "Don't withdraw, and don't be cynical. Stop complaining—engage people and be good citizens." God's surprising promise was that the welfare of Babylon would determine the Jewish people's welfare.

The word "welfare" is the Hebrew word *shalom*. It's often translated "peace," but it means a lot more than a happy, contented feeling. In an article about sin and grace, seminary president and professor Cornelius Plantinga Jr. observes,

In the Bible, shalom means universal flourishing, wholeness, and delight—a rich state of affairs in which natural needs are satisfied and natural gifts fruitfully employed, a state of affairs that inspires joyful wonder as its Creator and Savior opens doors and welcomes the creatures in whom he delights. Shalom, in other words, is the way things ought to be.[2]

In a widely diverse society, we're bound to have significant differences in the way we see people and issues. Too often, we focus on our disagreements instead of the things we can celebrate together. We shouldn't be surprised when we see people finding fault with those around them. If you think we have gripes against people in our culture, think about being an exile under the people who destroyed your homeland. It's these people God referred to when He said, "Work for their shalom." If these were God's instructions to the Jewish people living in Babylon, can't we do better than we're doing to love people who disagree with us?

Disagreement isn't the end of the world. It's not even close. In fact, it can lead to great conversations. We need to take small steps by asking people who hold different convictions to share their reasoning, and then listen. As we listen, we shouldn't be thinking about a great zinger that will slay them. The goal isn't to defeat them; it's to understand them, to communicate that we value them, and to assure them that we want a relationship—even if we disagree. And don't misunderstand: I'm not saying we have to agree with other people. But the question is, How do they feel when we part from one another? Do they feel valued and understood? Or do they feel attacked and belittled?

We also take small steps by refusing to participate in another person's rants. We don't "like" a snarky comment, and we don't jump in to inflame a friend who is hot about immigration, gun rights, gay marriage, an opinion on a restaurant, or any other topic.

And we take small steps by doing specific things to relieve suffering, soothe fears, and provide resources for those in need—those who live down the street and those who live across town. Jesus doesn't expect us to do everything, but He expects us to do something. And if we do something for the people near us, God will expand our borders. At least some of us will find ourselves loving people far from home. First, though, let's focus on those who are close by.

I talked to a friend who is connected to the foster care system, and he told me a shocking statistic. He said, "Chris, we don't need everybody in every church in America to foster a child. We only need one person from each church to step up. Today, there are about 443,000 kids in the program,[3] and there are about 384,000 churches.[4] If one person in each of them would find the heart to care for a child, we'd have a home for almost every child." That seems eminently doable.

> Jesus doesn't expect us to do everything, but He expects us to do something.

In Your Lap

I'm not suggesting that you start a nonprofit and raise a million dollars. (That's a couple of chapters later. Just kidding.) I'm only suggesting that you enlist your family or a few friends and brainstorm what you might do to make a difference in a few people's lives. You might find the money for ten bikes for foster kids. You might cut the grass for a neighbor who's in the hospital. You might bake cookies for the people at the local police station or firehouse. The options are endless.

Passion is almost always matched with need. In other words, we usually find ways to care for people by using the talents and resources we already have in our laps. Those who are skilled with their hands will want to help someone with plumbing or electrical work or tree trimming. An artist will want to decorate someone's room or paint a portrait. A person who came out of foster care will probably have a heart for lonely kids. Someone with a heart for the elderly will find ways to make a senior's life happier.

One of my favorite stories about someone who looked around and realized she could use the opportunity God had already put in her lap is about a dress designer. She designs and makes high-end prom dresses to sell in the finest retail shops, but she noticed that a lot of girls couldn't afford a nice dress . . . or any dress. She has donated hundreds of gorgeous, unique dresses for her church to give to girls who can't afford even a plain one. She started small, and as other ladies caught the vision, they now also give hair appointments, manicures, makeup, shoes, and other accessories for girls to go to proms. A grandmother wept as her granddaughter dressed because she could never have afforded to make such a dream come true for her. Do you think this generosity had any kingdom impact on that grandmother and her granddaughter? Of course it did! This was a way to love them that spoke volumes about the kindness, attention, and joy of Jesus.

Ask your family or a few friends to get together, then pray, brainstorm, pick a way to care, make a plan, and do it. Look at what's already in your lap that other people may need, and when you give it to them, smile. They'll never forget your love.

Jesus didn't call us to be a subculture the rest of the world can simply dismiss as irrelevant; He calls us to be a counterculture— people whose love shatters misconceptions about God and whose courage changes communities.

THINK ABOUT IT

1. How would you have felt if you had been the little boy whose lunch became a banquet? What was his role in the miracle? Why did Jesus involve him?

2. Do you agree or disagree with the statement "Miracles follow action"? Why?

3. Jesus said "Love one another" over and over again. Why do you think this is so important to Him?

4. What difference does it make to assume that sullen or scowling people have hurts that haven't healed yet?

5. What would it mean for Christians to work for the shalom of everyone in the culture, especially those who oppose them politically? Do you think that's even possible? Why or why not?

PRAY ABOUT IT

Thank God that He wants to involve you in the greatest enterprise the world has ever known—to extend His kingdom throughout your community and the world. Ask Him to give you an idea of how you can start small.

DO IT

What is your first step? Who will you ask to join you? When will you meet? When will you take action? Do it today . . . or at least tomorrow.

make it happen

Those in the circle of Christ had no doubt of his love; those in our circles should have no doubt about ours.

—Max Lucado

Pastor Adam Smith leads the South Hills campus in Corona, California. He conducted a LWYL Saturday and had asked the principal of a local school if she'd like them to redecorate their teachers' lounge. The team leader made sure all of the paint and supplies were ready when everyone arrived, and Adam joined the team. Together they worked hard, and in only a few hours the room started to look beautiful. In the middle of the morning, one of the school administrators dropped by to see the progress. She then went into the office and told the principal, "Do you know who is here right now? The pastor is in there with his whole team!" The next day, she had tears running down her cheeks as she reported at church, "The most impressive thing was that the entire church staff showed up to work on the lounge."

Scott Nalley is the pastor of Bridgeway Church in Fairfield, California, which has held several Love Where You Live events. They struck gold when they came up with the idea of "Laundry Love." Team members show up at local laundromats with rolls of quarters, detergent, and dryer sheets. They offer to pay for anyone's laundry, but that's not all: they also take donuts and coffee for people to enjoy. When the people ask, "Why are you doing this?" they respond, "We just want to bring a smile to your face and make this task a little more pleasant." Not long after the first time the team members served this way, three families that had been at the laundromat showed up in church.

Brian DeTalente, pastor of Refuge Christian Church in Evansville, Indiana, created a partnership with an organization that serves veterans to spruce up their landscaping. The executive director wrote to the team leader, "I want to thank you and your team for serving last Saturday. It was such an amazing transformation pulled off by the power of 10 people who gave up a Saturday morning sleep-in to show some worthy veterans that we care. High fives to you all and thanks a million for helping us realize this project."

One of the veterans had stopped by that morning to see what was going on. He was so inspired by the changes and the effort of the team that he immediately drove to the store to buy some extra supplies, including bags of stones and mulch. When he got back, he pitched in to help by spreading mulch in the flower bed. He remarked to one of the people on the team, "You people have changed my whole outlook on life today!" And they must have done a really good job. When one of the organization's volunteers saw the transformation, she cried . . . in a good way!

Things to Know before You Go

When churches mobilize their people to get involved in meeting the needs of the community, amazing things happen. We don't have to wait for a plague to ravage America for Christians to stand out and make a difference! Actually, the nagging problems in people's lives are often widespread, chronic, and debilitating—much like a plague. As we prepare to serve, we need to think clearly, pray hard, plan well, and mobilize many. We need to focus on the things that promise success.

> When churches mobilize their people to get involved in meeting the needs of the community, amazing things happen.

First, we need to learn three important lessons. When I talk to pastors about implementing Love Where You Live on a Saturday or a couple of Saturdays, I begin with some of the main points we saw when Jesus told the disciples, "You feed them," as they looked at twenty thousand hungry people far from the nearest takeout:

1. Stop asking Jesus to solve problems He wants you to solve.
2. Small acts of kindness matter . . . and they matter a lot!
3. Use the resources God has already put in your hands.

Second, we need a reality check. Many organizations in the community, especially governmental organizations like the Department of Parks and Rec, probably aren't going to throw their doors open wide when we offer to help. The reason is simple: they've been burned too often. Churches have overpromised and underdelivered. Their commitments took up valuable administrative time in the offices of these organizations, and the results weren't worth it. There are plenty of activities we can do that don't require coordination (or at least much coordination) with any agencies, but when we try to work with city officials and large nonprofits, we often have to patiently break down walls of suspicion others have built.

For instance, a number of church leaders have made appointments with mayors, city council members, the heads of Parks and Rec, and leaders of major organizations like the Red Cross and asked, "How can we help?" Quite often the response has been, "We're good." These church leaders were surprised until they found out that other churches before them had offered assistance but dropped the ball.

This isn't a rare occurrence. In fact, I'd say it's the norm. We're wise to anticipate some resistance and to work hard to build credibility, often by starting with a small project or two to prove ourselves before getting cooperation to launch a major effort. Ironically, we have to work hard to earn trust so we can give selflessly. We're coming to the plate with two strikes against us, so we'd better choke up and take a short swing to make sure we connect with the first pitch. Building credibility takes persis-

> The day we plant the seed isn't the day we eat the fruit.

tence and patience. The day we plant the seed isn't the day we eat the fruit.

As Love Where You Live becomes part of the church's culture, people in the community develop a different perception of the church. Instead of seeing us as takers, they see us as givers. Doing good markets the church because doing good is always inherently attractive.

Making It Happen

To this point in the book, we've been conceptual and theological. Now I want to be very practical. Let me get down to brass tacks of Love Where You Live.

1. Find the right leader and a great team.

Identify those who have a heart for hurting people and who are already taking initiative to care for others. Your staff or board members probably can help identify those people. Get them together and share the vision for Love Where You Live. Explain the concept and the process, and ask them to join the Love Where You Live leadership team. Pick someone as the coordinator who has the heart and administrative abilities to make it happen. And let me be brutally honest: some of the people who have a tender heart for those in need aren't, to be charitable, administratively gifted. You can't afford to have someone in charge who can't manage tasks, people, schedules, and details. Compassion and administration aren't necessarily mutually exclusive, but in my experience they definitely tend to come from different directions. Of course, it's wonderful if you have someone who is a blend of both.

Each of the people on the team also needs to have administrative skills. These people will be the "boots on the ground" to meet with leaders of nonprofits and city agencies to coordinate service efforts, work with church staff to place small groups and individuals on LWYL teams, make sure the resources are the right ones and arrive on time, and continually communicate the vision and heart of Love Where You Live. (Is that asking too much? No, I don't think so.)

2. Identify three or more organizations.

Depending on the size of your church, select three to perhaps fifteen organizations as potential partners for the Saturday or two of Love Where You Live. Appoint one of the LWYL leaders or team members as the contact person to visit with the heads of these organizations (and the coordinator may go with the contact person) to ask if they want the church's assistance. If they do, you can find out how to assist them, share the vision of Love Where You Live, and together create a plan for the church to help on the days of outreach.

3. Schedule the event.

Either before or after talking with the leaders of organizations, set the dates for Love Where You Live. Some churches start with one Saturday in the fall or spring, but many schedule two consecutive Saturdays. This way, individuals and families that aren't available on one day can participate on the other. However, we've found that many people enjoy the first day so much that they're eager to dive in the next week too.

The LWYL leadership team should begin coordinating with the leaders of organizations several months before the event, and the announcements and promotions can begin in the church a month or so before it. This gives people time to talk to their small groups or families to determine which organization they want to serve, and they can sign up online on a Splash page or on cards in the services.

At least two weeks before the event, the team leader needs to communicate with the people who have signed up to reinforce the vision, clarify the expectations and the schedule, and remind them what to bring to the kickoff, where everyone gathers that morning.

On the LWYL Saturdays, it's important to have a kickoff at the beginning and a gathering at the end. The start and ending times may vary, but some churches provide a light breakfast beforehand and get together for a celebration afterward as bookends of the day. The breakfast gets people together so they can see how many are involved, and they can hear from the pastor or the LWYL coordinator about the importance of being the hands and feet of Jesus. Some of the resources will have already been delivered to the job sites, but people will bring whatever tools and supplies the leader of their outreach has told them to bring. After four hours, it's a good idea to get everyone together for a short celebration and share stories from the day. Don't take too long. You'll have time the next morning in church to share more stories.

4. Watch it grow.

You and your church don't need to sign your life away in a long-term, comprehensive commitment to Love Where You Live. Schedule one Saturday a few months away and see how it goes. If it's successful, schedule another one six months later. And maybe schedule two Saturdays in a row. You can grow as fast as it seems good and right to you. Schedule the event once a year, twice a year, once a quarter, or whatever works for your church and your community. There's no right or wrong about how many you do—as long as you're getting outside of the church to care for people.

Some churches coordinate their events with holidays and particular months. For instance:

- Do a "Love Others" event on Valentine's Day.
- Celebrate Earth Month in April and Foster Care Awareness Month in May.
- Honor parents on Mother's Day and Father's Day.
- Honor veterans on Memorial Day.
- Take time for teacher appreciation in August and September.
- Remember National First Responders' Day in September.
- Serve the homeless during Homeless Awareness Month in November.
- Feed the disadvantaged at Thanksgiving.

Our church had a special event for single moms on Mother's Day. We washed their cars while they sat in the Sunday morning service, we gave them gift cards from a nice restaurant where they could go that night, and we offered to take care of their children.

The goal is for serving the community to become completely normal—an established and valued tradition in your church. Some efforts are moderately effective, very few bomb, and many are spectacularly successful. Look for projects that cause the eyes of those who serve to light up as they talk about their day's experiences. As people in your church get involved, their hearts will lean toward particular ways to show love.

Many people care about kids, especially kids who don't have a stable home. When a church added "Foster Parents' Day Out" to their LWYL outreach efforts, one of the foster care leaders wrote to thank the church:

> I am completely speechless over today's Parent Day Out! Words cannot express the feeling I felt today. To actually see the "church" being Jesus' extended hands and love was amazing! You have raised the bar of what it means to have a Parent Day Out! Our families could not believe the gifts they were receiving! That has never happened before. Everything was excellent! Your people, the activities, the food, the fun . . . everything! My staff was so impressed by your team and how they treated our families. Thank you! Thank you for blessing our families and making them feel special and important. And thank you for all that you did for the kiddos. Fostering is not easy, but with people and churches like you, families feel the support, encouragement, and love.

Do you think this church made Foster Parents' Day Out a regular part of LWYL? If they hadn't, they'd have had an uprising on their hands!

5. Enlist families and small groups.

Part of the beauty of Love Where You Live is that it's an opportunity for people to work side by side as they help others. Most parents want to bring their kids (even small kids) to participate, even if it means they spend a lot of their time helping their kids work instead of working themselves. And these Saturdays are terrific opportunities for small groups to rub shoulders doing something outside a living room. Their work together deepens relationships, surfaces talents, enlists resources, and builds momentum for group involvement in the future.

As you promote a LWYL event, be sure to let people know they can sign up as families and groups. People in groups may choose different activities for any number of reasons, but it's good to offer them the opportunity to work together.

6. Brand it.

Part of the preparation is to create a unique brand for Love Where You Live in your church. For instance, our South Hills campus in Burbank, California, created T-shirts that said, "Love the 818." That's the area code for Burbank. They also created a website, Lovethe818.com, where people could get information and sign up to serve. The possibilities for branding your church's involvement are limitless . . . and essential to build an identity and momentum. The brand of "Love the [area code]" has caught on, so churches around the country are known in their communities for their efforts to "Love the 310," "Love the 515," and so on. The area code may not always work, but your community may have another identifying name, like the Bay Area or the Mid-Cities or the Triangle. The point is to find a way to brand your Love Where You Live.

On some churches' websites, the home page prominently features pictures of people wearing these T-shirts and holding a shovel or a paintbrush. It looks like it's going to catch on!

7. Prepare, prepare, prepare.

Love Where You Live works when motivated people have all the resources they need to accomplish specific tasks for an appreciative organization. For this to happen, people need to be recruited and placed on teams; they need to know what to bring; the organization needs to have specific tasks clearly identified; all the resources need to arrive before the teams get there; the team leader needs to be clear, calm, and confident before, during, and after the event; and it needs to start and end on time.

Does that sound like a tall order? It's not, if you have people who are administratively gifted. Let me put it another way: Love Where You Live is a complete and utter disaster if people don't catch a vision for how their investment of a Saturday morning will be genuinely effective in helping particular people, if the organization's leader doesn't have things for the team to do, if resources don't arrive on time, if the leader is a basket case, or if the event starts or ends late.

It's far better to have fewer activities that are led well than to have too many that are poorly led. It may sound more impressive to say, "We have twenty-five projects planned for our Love Where You Live Saturday," but if you only have competent leaders for six, you should only have six.

Each team leader needs to make sure to get the right resources for the job. Sometimes this takes considerable effort and expense. For instance, if you're going to landscape an area of a park, you may need to get a Bobcat or a rototiller on-site the day before to prepare the ground. You don't want a dozen people—parents and kids—standing around for three hours waiting for the ground to be prepared before they can plant a couple of bushes and a few flowers. And bushes and flowers aren't cheap. You'll need a reasonable budget and probably a limited scope of what can be done, and it may take two Saturdays to complete the job—or maybe two cycles of Love Where You Live.

Other activities, like painting a teachers' lounge, take a few gallons of paint (get plenty!), painter's tape, drop cloths, brushes and rollers, and cleanup supplies. A more extensive makeover of a teachers' lounge—complete with a fresh paint job, a new sofa, a plasma screen television, a couple of nice chairs, and a table—may cost $3,000 to $4,000. Taking brownies to people at a senior living center is easy and inexpensive, the baking can include children, and the seniors love it.

Love Where You Live events cost money. Aside from the supplies for each activity, the church may also provide breakfast and lunch for the participants. You may have someone underwrite this expense, but the church usually bears some of the cost. The question is simple: is it worth it? Can a small church take money out of an already stretched budget to care for people who probably won't put any money in the offering plate—ever? My answer, unsurprisingly, is "Absolutely!" It's worth it because it models the sacrificial heart of Jesus, it puts us in touch with people in need (people we have compassion for because we've been needy too), it enables the church to make a tangible difference in the community, it pulls on the heartstrings of everyone involved—servants and recipients, it builds momentum in the church, it identifies rising leaders, and it creates a positive image of the church among the people in the community.

> The question is simple: is it worth it?

8. Follow through.

It's not the most brilliant insight, but it's an absolutely essential truth: we need to do what we say we're going to do. Our credibility can be wonderfully enhanced among the people in our church as well as among the leaders of other organizations in the community if we follow through with our commitments, but we become one of "those churches" if we don't fulfill our commitments. This is why it's so important to have a LWYL coordinator who is administratively talented, and for each team leader to have the ability to plan, recruit, schedule, gather resources, and lead people with enthusiasm. I'm all for people having tender, compassionate hearts, but those in charge need to dot all the i's and cross all the t's.

If you fail to follow through at one elementary school, it's very likely that your reputation is shot throughout the school system. Leaders talk to each other, and principals at other schools will find out that you didn't do what you said you'd do. If the principal at the elementary school had teachers clear out all their stuff from the lounge and asked the janitor to work overtime to open doors and answer questions, but your team made a mess, didn't have supplies in time to finish the job, or didn't even show up, you'll make a strong impression—a really bad strong impression! Principals at other schools probably won't take the risk to open their doors to you any time soon.

The failure to organize also deflates the people who signed up but whose Saturday morning was wasted as they waited for supplies or wandered around from site to site. One of the most common planning concerns is childcare. Many families want their kids to join them in their serving activity, and it's great to have children and teenagers jump in to help. But parents with infants either show up and spend all their time caring for their child or don't come at all. Churches need to decide if they want to provide childcare or expect parents of infants and toddlers to figure it out on their own. Sometimes one or more of the people on a team can be asked to provide childcare on the job site. When our church pitched in to clean up a park, two of our team members played with the little kids at a nearby playground and gave them snacks. That's what worked for them. Each church and each team needs to figure out what works for them.

No matter what, make it fun, make it easy, make it meaningful, and make it effective.

Take the Lid Off!

What would it look like if the entire church got involved in Love Where You Live? What would it mean to take the lid off our expectations? As you expand the number of organizations that become partners, virtually everyone in the church will find a good fit. There's no limit to the creative ideas. Here are just a few organizations and activities to consider:

Local Nonprofits
- Homeless shelters
- Housing organizations
- Foster care agencies
- Ronald McDonald House
- Veteran housing
- Pregnancy centers
- Adopting a family or a giving tree for Christmas

Local Schools

- Donating staff donuts and coffee
- Donating staff lunches
- Remodeling the teachers' lounge
- Landscaping
- Helping get classrooms prepared the week before school starts
- Doing a phys ed supply drive (create an Amazon wish list)

Local Government

- Department of Parks and Recreation (cleanup days)
- Animal shelters
- Police and fire departments
- Senior centers
- Organizing parades
- Hosting Christmas events
- Doing backpack drives
- Helping at marathons (serving, supplying water, etc.)

Local Events

- Hosting single mom events
- Paying for people's laundry
- Doing prom dress giveaways
- Organizing blood drives
- Hosting events to support local organizations (for example, hosting a movie night showing *Captain Underpants* and asking people to bring undergarments for a local nonprofit)

Yes, it takes some work. Yes, it takes some time, funding, and other resources. Yes, it may even take some people away from serving inside the church for a while, but the benefits of Love Where You Live are enormous. Make sure you keep the goal crystal clear—for you and everyone involved. Accomplishing anything significant requires sacrifice. If you're not willing to sacrifice for what you want, then what you want becomes the sacrifice. Think it through, pray for direction, and plan diligently. If you find the right person as the coordinator of Love Where You Live, and that person finds the right people to lead each project team, you'll make a difference in the lives of hundreds if not thousands of people, your church will be known for its compassion, those who serve will tap into the heart of Jesus, and people will come to your church who would never have considered coming before.

> If you're not willing to sacrifice for what you want, then what you want becomes the sacrifice.

Does all this sound too good to be true? Not really. I know it's true because I've seen it so many times.

THINK ABOUT IT

1. Why is it essential to have administratively gifted people leading your Love Where You Live effort? What might happen if you didn't have people with this talent in charge?

2. In your church, who are some people who would be terrific on this team? Explain your answer.

3. What are some organizations and activities you can consider for your first (or your next) Love Where You Live event? What's attractive about each of these?

4. How many LWYL events is just right? How will you decide which ones to focus on? How will you match leaders, organizations, and funding sources?

5. Describe the importance of follow-through with the organizations you want to help and with your people.

PRAY ABOUT IT

Ask God for wisdom about selecting leaders, open doors to serve, resources to make a difference, and the joy of seeing the impact on people you serve.

DO IT

Take the steps outlined in this chapter. Pick a leader, develop a team, pick a date, select organizations, and get going.

8

woven into the fabric

> Darkness cannot drive out darkness: only light can
> do that. Hate cannot drive out hate: only love can
> do that.
>
> —Martin Luther King Jr.

Quite often, something clicks. Dave Stewart's church in Burbank conducted a Love Where You Live outreach at a school
to redecorate the teachers' lounge. That went really well, so
they were asked back to work on the landscaping. Word got
out, and principals at other schools contacted the church to
get on their list for the next event. Soon, the school district
viewed the church as a trusted ally. Dave was asked to speak at
a high school commencement, church members got to know
teachers and became volunteer aides, and when tragedy struck
and a student was killed in a car accident, Dave and the church
were seen as the first call for help. The principal asked Dave to
go to the home of the parents to console them. It was a high
honor. In situations like this, when a lot of people are expected

for a memorial service, a principal usually calls the pastor of the biggest church in town. This church wasn't the biggest, but they had become the most valued, the most trusted, the most comforting, the most loving. The relationship between the school system and the church isn't a formal partnership, but the informal one is strong and meaningful.

Of course, it's not just school systems. As Love Where You Live makes a difference in senior citizens' homes, group homes for people with special needs, trauma centers, foster care homes, and a host of nonprofits, the life of the church is gradually woven into the fabric of the community. The activities don't have to be dramatic or expensive, but they can lead to something special.

For instance, a family who took brownies to seniors in a LWYL event developed a relationship with several of them, so they go back every month with a big plate of cookies, brownies, and cupcakes—and they sit around and enjoy talking with the seniors. This family is a bright light to these men and women, and everyone delights in giving and receiving love.

After a few months, the seniors asked, "Would you lead a church service for us each Sunday? We have a conference room we can use."

The dad responded, "I don't think I can do it, but I'll find someone who can." He asked a man who teaches a Bible study to come teach each week. He found someone to lead the singing, and they dove in. The first week, there were about twenty people. By the third week, the room was packed with fifty seniors!

When these connections happen, we aren't just doing projects *for* people; we're doing life *with* them. This is the point where the church has a profound impact on individuals, on community leaders, and on the culture of the city.

Beyond the Event

Don't miss this point: Love Where You Live may begin with isolated projects, but the goal is to develop ongoing relationships that continually make a difference in your community. Every organization has a USP: an ultimate strategic position. Amazon sells almost every item we can imagine, and they can have it at your door tomorrow—or even today! Companies that make cars, refrigerators, clothes, and every other product, as well as companies that provide services like banking and the internet, have to position themselves as unique and better than their competition.

Is your church's ultimate strategic position that you have great teaching or great worship? Every church makes these promises, and many of them are very similar. But there's something you can do to set your church apart. I guarantee you that very few, if any, churches in your community are doing things that make them indispensable to schools, nonprofits, government agencies, hospitals, and group homes. Love Where You Live gives your church the opportunity to be the greatest resource in your city . . . and to be known for being the greatest resource.

If you don't believe me, call a school principal and ask how many churches have redecorated rooms or landscaped the front entrance. Call a police or fire department and ask how many churches regularly show their appreciation. Call a nonprofit and ask how many churches have contributed manpower in a significant way. Many churches give money and donations of clothes to homeless shelters and nonperishable items to food pantries, but relatively few of them build real connections with the leaders of these organizations. Don't get me wrong: this isn't a competition. If several churches in your area are sharing their love in the neighborhoods of your city, that's fantastic! There are more than enough needs for all to be involved. But I haven't seen very many churches make more than momentary forays outside the fortress walls of their buildings. Be the ones that love enough to invest yourselves in the community.

Let me make some suggestions as you move from projects to relationships.

1. *Be consistent.*

    Relationships thrive on consistent and meaningful interactions. If your people can show up once a month at a senior living center, homeless shelter, trauma center, or police station, the people there will count the days before the next visit. Don't make promises you don't keep. If you make a commitment to be there, be there.

2. *Trust God for one or two partners.*

    Your church may have five, ten, or more service projects on a Love Where You Live Saturday, but your leaders probably won't have the bandwidth to build strong relationships with the leaders of all these organizations. Pick one or two, make sure a competent leader picks up the ball for each one and runs with it, and see how the relationships develop. As your leadership team grows, as the number of your LWYL opportunities increases, and as you sense a community leader will be a good partner, pick another one.

3. *Connect with leaders.*

Ask your key leaders who are assigned to work with particular organizations to make a special effort to get to know the leaders of those organizations. This commitment requires someone to take responsibility for the relationship, probably someone on the LWYL leadership team—perhaps a key volunteer. If that person is you, how do you get to know the leader and build a relationship? Not by walking up and saying, "I'm curious. What's your deepest secret?" They'll run and hide! Instead, send a note after a LWYL event to thank the person for coordinating with you, find out their birthday and send a card, take a small gift at Christmas, and send a note for special events like the beginning or the end of the school year.

I'm recommending that you be a friend, not be weird. Don't overdo your initiative, but tastefully and openhandedly communicate messages that you care. Consider serving in small ways outside the LWYL events. If you've decorated a room, take coffee and cookies a few weeks later, and maybe once a month over the next year. Be creative, be wise, but be involved.

I've seen it work magic. When a person takes the time to write a note on the special days for a community leader in a school, an agency, a fire station, a police station, or anywhere else in the city, bonds of friendship are built and trust grows.

I've found it's best to have senior pastors or campus pastors connect with city leaders. In relating to nonprofits, I've seen some small groups "adopt" an organization and provide regular assistance beyond the

LWYL events, and of course some individuals are so moved by their own involvement on a Saturday morning that they want to regularly volunteer to serve an organization.

What's the cost? Maybe ten dollars for cards and postage for the year, or if you're extravagant, fifty dollars for cards and a couple of bouquets of flowers. It doesn't take much money to close the gap between these leaders and our churches, but it takes a little time, a little money, and a lot of heart.

4. *Automate the important.*

I make a point of being deeply involved in this level of Love Where You Live, but it's a challenge. Let's be honest. Some of us are temperamentally inclined to remember birthdays, anniversaries, the dog's favorite treat, and where everyone went on their last vacation. And some of us aren't. Those who naturally remember the details of others' lives and delight to send notes to them are magnificent, but I'm not one of them. I need help. In fact, I need a lot of help. If I hadn't figured out a way to organize and orchestrate my interactions with community leaders, they wouldn't have happened.

To make sure I don't forget my commitment to send cards, I put dates and prompts in my phone . . . on repeat. The prompts remind me to mail a note a few days before Christmas, the leader's birthday, Father's Day or Mother's Day, and for those in the school district, the start of the school year and the last day of the school year. I always have stationery or holiday cards on hand, so it only takes a few minutes to write a note, address it, and put it in the mail. Does it matter? Of course it does. How much do you appreciate it when people remember to do the little things that let you know they care?

5. *Love the people they love.*

Now it's time for the graduate course in building relationships with city officials and nonprofit leaders. When we pay special attention to the people they love, they're amazed, and they greatly appreciate it. For instance, if, over the course of getting to know an official, you discover that her five-year-old likes Skittles and her eight-year-old likes Snickers, bring those when you visit. Or if a principal raves about his administrative assistant, the next time you drop by his office, give the assistant a gift card from a local coffee shop and a note that says, "Bob told me you're the best. He appreciates you so much. Here's a small gift to show how much I appreciate you too." That's the kind of thing I do with leaders and their staff as I build relationships with them.

You don't have to be James Bond to figure out who's important to the leaders in your community. When you meet with them, ask them to tell you about the family picture on their desk or the vacation shot on the wall. And listen. Don't give them the third degree. Just listen. You may discover their eyes light up when they talk about a son or daughter, or the picture brings up a painful memory and you can be a source of comfort.

A leader may have been only a name and a number when Love Where You Live began, but now he or she is becoming a friend. That's how friendships work. In *The Four Loves*, C. S. Lewis got to the heart of true friendship:

> Friendship arises out of mere Companionship when two or more of the companions discover that they have in common some insight or interest or even taste which the others do not share and which, till that moment, each believed to be his own unique treasure (or burden). The typical expression of opening Friendship would be something like, "What? You too? I thought I was the only one." . . . It is when two such persons discover one another, when, whether with immense difficulties and semi-articulate fumblings or with what would seem to us amazing and elliptical speed, they share their vision—it is then that Friendship is born. And instantly they stand together in an immense solitude.[1]

Is it possible to have this kind of relationship with a community leader? It's uncommon, but it's certainly possible. When we move toward others with genuine interest, defenses drop, hard hearts melt, and we give and receive the gift of understanding. Even with the mayor.

Know This

I suspect that the person who might become the coordinator of the LWYL leadership team—and for that matter, each member of the team—isn't sitting around doing nothing right now. If they have the heart and skills necessary for these roles, they're already neck deep in effective ministry in your church. It's unreasonable to ask them to add these responsibilities to what they're already doing, so you (and they) need to think, pray, prioritize, and make some hard decisions. Perhaps someone currently serving under them can step up and take their place, or perhaps someone new can step in and step up. Be aware, though, that LWYL will almost certainly necessitate some reorganization and reassignment. However, the benefits are well worth the temporary discomfort of change.

For several chapters now, I'm pretty sure you've wanted to ask, "Chris, what about sharing the gospel with people at LWYL sites? You haven't said much about that." Great question. I'm glad you finally asked. I'm all for taking opportunities to communicate the life-changing message of the gospel of grace. However, in this culture of in-your-face messages, it's important that we earn the right to open our mouths. We earn it by serving selflessly, demonstrating that we care about people, and communicating that we don't see them as "targets" for our gospel bullets. When they see us serving with no strings attached, they're often surprised and more than a little impressed, especially as we work with officials in city government and leaders of nonprofits. They're pressured by all kinds of interest groups, so their radar is finely tuned to pick up anything that looks like they're being treated

> LWYL will almost certainly necessitate some reorganization and reassignment. However, the benefits are well worth the temporary discomfort of change.

indispensable church

as things instead of people. Genuine love earns the opportunity to sensitively and appropriately tell people about Jesus.

When we build relationships with people over several LWYL events, we don't have to feel pushed to share the gospel right away. We can take our time, demonstrate love, and look for the right time and place. And then we can say, "I'd like to tell you about the most meaningful thing in my life. It's my relationship with Jesus. Would you mind if I told you about Him?" This gives people the chance to say yes or no, and we respect their decision. If they're willing to listen, we need to be able to share our testimony of how we came to faith in Jesus and how His forgiveness, love, and power have changed us. The goal isn't to get someone to pray a quick prayer so we can count them as a convert; the goal is for them to grasp the wonder of God's grace in Jesus' payment for their sins on the cross.

Make sure you don't rush the process. Patiently answer any questions, and if you don't know the answer, say, "I don't know. I'll find out and get back to you." It's better to focus on building the relationship and finding out more about the person. They may talk about a struggle in their life or their family, and you can say something like, "Our church often addresses problems like this, and I've found the answers to be very helpful. If you get a chance, give our church a try."

> Jesus taught people about grace, forgiveness, and the kingdom of God, but always in the context of connecting and caring.

Love Where You Live gives us wonderful opportunities to follow the example of Jesus to share the gospel as we love

152

people. Yes, Jesus taught people about grace, forgiveness, and the kingdom of God, but always in the context of connecting and caring. That's the model for us too.

Our Partnerships

At our church, we've made a point of making a strong connection with the local Parks and Rec. We started with one LWYL serve day, and the relationship has grown so that they see us as a valuable partner in town. The work we do for them usually doesn't require an advanced engineering degree. Anyone can do it, as long as they don't fall off the side of the hill as they pull weeds and chop brush. One of the benefits of this work is that it both builds a great relationship with the city and is an easy place to put any extra people who haven't previously signed up but show up at the breakfast on the day we serve. People can work at their own pace, and when we're finished for the day, we can look at the flower beds, fields, or hillside and see what we've done. It's gratifying. Young people enjoy doing physical labor together.

This work can open doors to other departments and agencies in the city or county. From my experience, I've seen that it doesn't take long for the church to get a reputation for dependability, and leaders welcome the church's assistance. Some of the churches that have built a tradition of Love Where You Live have been recognized by their communities. They've received awards for citizenship and service, which is a lot more positive than for the community to assume that all Christians are hypocrites! When people in the community see and feel the love we have for them, they'll probably want to know more about the source of that love.

The same principles that apply to relationships with the leaders of Parks and Rec apply to connections with members of the city council, the mayor's office, or schools: be consistent, start small and trust God for one or two partner agencies, connect with leaders, automate the important, and love the people they love.

One of the churches that has held several Love Where You Live events developed a long and strong relationship with their local Parks and Rec. The church wanted to use a stadium for a citywide Easter service, but the city hadn't allowed a church to use it for almost two decades. The pastor called the head of Parks and Rec and said, "I know you don't usually rent the stadium to churches, but it would be perfect for our Easter celebration. I wonder if—"

"When do you want it?"

"Uh, well, just on that Sunday morning."

"Done."

"That's, uh . . . great. How much is the rent for one day?"

"For other organizations, $5,000. For you, nothing."

That's a tangible result of the intentional connection the pastor and his church had made with the leader of Parks and Rec. And by the way, on that Easter morning nearly one hundred people trusted in Jesus and entered His kingdom.

Sometimes unusual opportunities present themselves, and if we're part of a network of relationships, we can serve in unique ways. One of the pastors whose church has built strong connections with their school district through Love Where You Live told me this story:

Teachers in our local district all apply for various grants. Many of these grants are approved, but obviously they can't all be approved. There is a special education teacher at the school where our campus meets whose grant application was not funded. It was a request for funding to provide flexible seating for his students, which has a significant impact on the way special needs students are able to learn. Our church rallied together to fully fund his grant. He was obviously overwhelmed and came on a Sunday to thank our church. He's not a Christian, but he couldn't hold back his emotion as he thanked the church for the way they cared for him *and* for the students that he loves so much.

Is developing connections with community leaders a church growth strategy or the natural development of relationships as we serve them? Is it intentional and planned, or does it just happen as we get to know each other? The answer, of course, is yes! These relationships begin with a sense of direction to accomplish a plan, but as soon as they get going, the strategy becomes secondary. We have the opportunity to touch people throughout our community, but we need leaders to open doors for us. Love is the key.

THINK ABOUT IT

1. Who are some community leaders you know? What is their impression of the churches in town? How can you tell? What do you think formed their opinion?

2. If your church hasn't had a Love Where You Live Saturday yet, how would you prioritize your list of the nonprofits and agencies as possible partners for the event?

3. If your church has had at least one event, which additional community and nonprofit leaders do you think would make good partners? How can you build relationships with these leaders without them thinking they're no more than a project to you? How will this help to weave you and your church into the fabric of the community?

4. What are your best ways of connecting and keeping up with people? What would be the benefits of automating the important contacts?

5. Who loves the people you love? What difference does it make to you?

PRAY ABOUT IT

If you're a pastor, ask God to lead you to establish a genuine friendship with a community leader. If you're a church member or attender, ask Him to give you meaningful connections with nonprofit agencies or officials in city government.

DO IT

Talk to your pastor or your LWYL coordinator or team leader, and determine if you're the right person to take the initiative to build a relationship with a leader in the community. If so, do it, and do it with authenticity, compassion, and wisdom.

9

create a movement

God is not keeping score with our bank accounts, our trophies, or what people are saying about us. The only thing that matters is how we spend our love.

—Alice Camille

Love Where You Live can be effective as a one-off event, but it can be so much more. When people see God use them to change lives—when they see the look on the face of a person who feels loved for the first time in a long time, or maybe ever—they want to do it again . . . and again. And church leaders want to do it again because they see the incredible results as their people take action to make a difference in their communities.

Love Where You Live:

Attracts new people to the church.
Raises up new leaders.

Releases generosity.

Motivates new volunteers.

Gives your church a great reputation in the community.

Creates shared enthusiasm.

Puts people in touch with the heart of Jesus.

In other words, it becomes a powerful movement, and movements take on a life of their own.

In 2014, someone thought of a unique angle to raise money for Madi Rogers, a Tennessee toddler who was suffering from juvenile diabetes. The money would buy a service dog for her. The person who began the challenge asked people to jump into cold water (it was March in Tennessee, so every lake, river, pool, and pond was cold!) and donate to the cause. Each participant tagged the next person to jump and give, and it caught on. One of the first videos posted on YouTube appeared on March 8, and a few months later, it had over fifty thousand views.

By June, the "Cold Water Challenge" had morphed into the "Ice Bucket Challenge." Motocross racer Jeremy McGrath posted an Instagram video of pouring ice water on his head and challenging rapper Vanilla Ice and two famous athletes who were his friends, golfer Rickie Fowler and racer Jimmy Johnson, to do it or pay $100 to the ALS Association. Most of the people who accepted the challenge did both, and many of them posted their own videos of having a bucket of ice water dumped on their heads. It was easy, it was fun, and it was for a good cause. The organization raised almost four times as much money that year than it had in the previous year.[1]

Movements Come in All Sizes

Movements may be as consequential as the civil rights movement or as simple as the impulse to buy a pair of TOMS shoes so a person a world away will get a pair. Today, we can find groups of people who are motivated to take stands about bullying, Black Lives Matter, Blue Lives Matter, women's rights, the Me Too movement, political convictions, the environment, and a host of other issues. In every case, a cause captures hearts and transforms behavior. Invariably, those who get involved feel a connection to people who are in need, and they're motivated to move beyond their normal, safe, everyday world to take the risk to care.

Movements are like rivers. A bucket of water doesn't have much of an impact on geography, but even a relatively slow river carves the landscape, breaking down banks, depositing sediments, and changing its course. Momentum has a powerful impact.

Movements Start Small

Movements usually don't start with a bang; they start with a pop. Love Where You Live is seldom birthed as a full-blown strategy in a church. Most church leaders get one foot wet with a single Saturday, then have two Saturdays, then two Saturdays twice a year. By that time, they've formed informal or formal partnerships with nonprofits and government agencies. People in the church realize that serving the community is entirely normal, and they bring their passion and creativity to accelerate the efforts to make a difference. Community leaders value the church's contributions, so they open their doors to more opportunities. The mayor trusts the pastor and the people of the church. The police and fire departments see the church as a partner in serving the city. Principals and teachers feel supported. Veterans, seniors, disabled people, and those who are poor and homeless realize someone sees them, someone cares, and someone is stepping into their lonely world with tangible aid.

> Movements usually don't start with a bang; they start with a pop.

The people who receive care want to find out more about the people who love them, so they ask what motivates them, and some come to church. Each event is a tributary, and gradually the river gets larger and more powerful. Compassion and resources break down barriers and cut new paths of hope for people inside and outside the church.

How does LWYL gain momentum and become a real movement? In many ways, but certainly by telling compelling, vivid stories.

The Power of Stories

People go to movies and read novels because they love stories—the more drama the better. Similarly, we capture hearts when we work hard to tell the stories of how God uses Love Where You Live. It's important to prepare people and resources for the Saturday events, but it's just as important to craft the narrative before, during, and after each one. I recommend that you include someone on the LWYL leadership team who is in charge of communication, specifically communication to the people in the church. This person needs a camera, a winsome personality, the ability to draw out details in interviews, and some savvy about social media. The LWYL communications director may also have contacts with local media outlets who want to cover the events.

A church in Hollywood, California, launched Love Where You Live, and they quickly discovered they were swimming upstream. Many of the leaders of schools, agencies, and non-profits were reluctant to participate (if not defiant) because churches hadn't delivered on their promises in the past. The pastor was undaunted. On the first Saturday, about twenty people came to serve in two projects; the next time, forty people served in six projects. A year later, his team scheduled twenty projects for the one hundred people who signed up. As of this writing, their last Love Where You Live event sent 320 people to serve in forty-five different places in the city. The movement caught on and grew for many reasons, but one of them was that the pastor knows the power of stories. He made it a high priority to select the right person to capture the stories, and he devoted time in worship services to tell them—and the stories moved hearts.

During this growth, the movement spawned creative T-shirts and bumper stickers. The city gave the church an award for their contribution to the good of the community. Splash pages told more stories than could be shared on Sunday mornings, and the enthusiasm kept growing.

The principle is simple and powerful: tell stories about the behaviors you want repeated. And don't wait a

> The principle is simple and powerful: tell stories about the behaviors you want repeated.

week to interview people. Have your communications person (or team, if your LWYL efforts have grown and you need more people so you can tell more stories) at the breakfast to show the enthusiasm and on the job sites to record people as they're working. You might even show some of these videos and still shots when you get everybody back together for a quick lunch to share what happened that morning, but certainly you can show some videos the next morning in church, on social media, and months later as you fire up the crowd to sign up in the weeks before the next LWYL Saturday.

The Rock and the Flywheel

In my years of observing people who are trying to accomplish goals, I've noticed a tried-and-true principle: if you push a rock uphill and decide to take a break, the rock won't. A few pastors have told me, "Yeah, we had a great time doing Love Where You Live, but the next year we were in a building project and didn't do it. I think our people have lost interest." Movements don't last without constant input of energy. That's how a flywheel works. At first, a lot of effort is required to move it just a little, but each revolution becomes a little easier and a little quicker. After a while, the same amount of energy propels the flywheel much faster. But at the point energy is withdrawn, the wheel begins to slow down, and if more energy isn't applied, it'll grind to a halt. That's what happened to the enthusiasm and drive at these pastors' churches.

Speed at the beginning of the process of change isn't as important as persistence. We may have grand visions for the future, but we need to pay attention to the next step . . . and then the next. As a leader, sometimes you have to go slower to eventually go farther.

Serving Will Become the Norm

As you start small, do the little things well, tell great stories, build relationships with community leaders, prove you're trustworthy, love the people they love, send cards, and put people in positions to see God change lives, people already in your church will experience a culture shift; people who are new to your church will believe serving the city is just what Christians do; and people in the community will come to your church because they want to join others whose love touches hearts, meets needs, and changes the trajectory of lives. If serving is the river, every person who is already in or gets in will be swept downstream. The church's culture will be defined by love—not isolation, not suspicion, not bickering over petty things, and not trying to look spiritual without heart change. There's something about serving that sifts our motivations, surfaces our passions, and motivates us to experience the love of God more so that we can express His love to others.

Leaders in the community will recognize the contribution your church makes, and after a while, your reputation will attract groups that want your help. Instead of you knocking on doors and begging for opportunities to serve, the leaders of organizations will be knocking on your door, and you'll need to vet them to choose the ones that are the best fit for your church.

Any Church, Every Church

Love Where You Live fits into the strategy of every church in every stage of growth, because it's not based on any kind of gimmick. It's the heart of God for people. Let's look at the range of stages.

- *Church plants* can have Love Where You Live Saturdays for their launch team even before they open the doors for the first service, or as a kickoff series. This makes a dramatic statement about the church being *for* the city, not just *in* the city. The pastor of our church plant in Dana Point, California, sent me this report:

  > Love Where You Live was our first series, and only a few weeks in, we were able to welcome the city manager of Dana Point as part of Love Where You Live. He and his wife (who is a school principal) were impressed that we care about our community so much that we intentionally designated an entire series to it. He thanked me and South Hills Church for choosing Dana Point to plant this campus!
  >
  > What better way to kick off our church than by loving the people in our community!

- In *young churches*, the pastor and many of the leaders are really busy setting up in a school each Sunday and trying to get programs off the ground, so it's easy for them to think they can't possibly add one more program. But they can. In fact, they really need to. They need to make sure the culture of their church isn't so inwardly focused that they lose sight of their

God-given role in the community. Yes, they'll have
to prioritize, and yes, they'll need to take some very
competent people away from what they're already
doing, but creating a loving, giving culture is central to
the kingdom Jesus wants to establish on earth. Quite
often a few people in these churches are exhausted, so
maybe the leaders need a better way to recruit, train,
place, and oversee people, so those who are tired aren't
the only ones actively serving.

- *Established churches* have a culture based on a history
  of growth, leadership changes, and struggles. Over
  the years, the board and members have come up with
  dozens, maybe hundreds, of ideas for programs, and
  many of them have become part of the church's life.
  Adding one more can seem like the proverbial straw
  that breaks the camel's back. The question is, does the
  "one more program" have the ability to accelerate positive change, or is it in fact just one more of probably
  too many?

  Love Where You Live gets people outside the cocoon
  of the church building and puts them in contact with
  people in need. For many believers, it's transforma-
  tive. For the churches, it's essential. In many cases, the
  people in these churches have been promoted to death.
  They've been told that this event or that class or this new
  building will make all the difference in the world, but
  it hasn't. Now they're skeptical when someone comes
  along with something new. That's okay. It's not the end
  of the world. At this point, the culture isn't as vibrant as
  it was when the church was young, but the skepticism

can be overcome. The pastor can find a coordinator who is passionate about Love Where You Live and communicates the vision with passion and clarity. In a church of three hundred, only a handful may show up on the first Saturday. If they have a great time and see God use them, those numbers will increase.

The growth chart for LWYL may be more gradual in established churches, but pastors and other leaders shouldn't get discouraged. Changing the way people think, feel, believe, prioritize, and act is never easy, especially if these habits have been entrenched for many years.

- In *churches on the decline*, Love Where You Live may be the last and best hope to turn the ship around. A new vision can breathe fresh life into a discouraged congregation. Getting involved in serving others just may distract people from the blaming, arguing, and pettiness that often is the poisonous atmosphere of churches on their way down. Instead of turning their guns on each other, they can direct their energies to care for those who are less fortunate and in desperate need, and they can see real change.

  I'm not making any promises. Ornery people may still argue about Love Where You Live instead of using it to serve gladly, but if they can expend their energies in compassion instead of complaints, good things can happen.

Spiritual movements don't just happen. They require two components: a combustible environment and the fire of the

Holy Spirit to ignite it. We, then, have two priorities: to create the infrastructure, schedule, programs, and relational networks in the community (the combustible environment), and pray like crazy that the Spirit of God will do what only He can do—melt hearts so they become compassionate, open doors of opportunity, give us courage to take risks to love people outside our normal range of connections, and reveal lives radically changed by God's love expressed through us. I don't think this is asking too much.

> Spiritual movements don't just happen. They require two components: a combustible environment and the fire of the Holy Spirit to ignite it.

The Long View

Remember, all of this isn't just to occupy our time on a Saturday morning. It's to make a difference in people's lives, in organizations, and in the entire city. A friend of mine, Dick Foth, says that churches can "own the city." He's not talking about a backroom power play at city hall. He means that we can have such a powerful influence of love on the city that leaders and citizens in the community look to us for wisdom, hope, and care. He has observed that in every city, no matter the size, only a handful of people really call the shots. These are the ones whose opinions matter . . . but these are the ones who are often the hardest to impress. They hear demands and complaints all the time. What they don't hear are openhanded offers to help, stories of effective action as people care for those who can't give back, and heartfelt gratitude. When they see that in us, they sit up and notice. If pastors will learn how to pastor the city as well as the church, they can become one of a handful of people with the strongest impact on the city.

The day will come when a crisis strikes people in leadership in the community. A tornado, hurricane, or fire causes destruction, a tragic accident kills and cripples, an unexpected illness or suicide takes someone they love far too early, or a son or daughter is in trouble. In those moments, these leaders become vulnerable, desperate, and open. If they see us as friends, they'll turn to us for help. It's a heavy responsibility and a high honor, but it's a role we'll never shoulder if we stay inside the church to manage our inward-focused programs.

Some pastors and other church leaders have been reading up to this point, and they have a few nagging questions. Some shake their heads and ask, "Chris, I'm already maxed out. How in the world can I add something like this to my schedule? Do you want me to get a divorce so I'll have more time, or do you expect me to get a divorce because I'm so busy?"

Very funny, but I get it. You're busy, I'm busy, we're all busy. I'm convinced that serving people in our communities is a priority, so I have to make some choices about the things I do, how I do them, and who I can get to help lead. In my experience and from the reports of many pastors who have implemented Love Where You Live, it's obvious that people in our churches are enthusiastic about serving. That's a double-edged sword: we're thrilled that so many are excited about it and want to participate, but it also means that it can't be pulled off in a slipshod way. Pray, talk to your leadership team, and look for people who can carry the load. Yes, you'll still have to cast vision, lead, and put out some fires along the way, but I'm convinced you'll see that it's worth it.

Many church leaders ask, "All this sounds great, but what if we can't afford the expense of Love Where You Live?"

Let me give several answers. First, many of the projects require very few tangible resources. People who are cleaning a park bring their own rakes and shovels. You may need to provide some huge plastic trash bags, but that's only a few bucks. Painting a room at a school or group home may cost fifty to one hundred dollars for the paint, and people can bring brushes and rollers from home if you need to save money. In other words, you can tailor your service projects to the activities that don't cost much.

Second, you can trust God to provide. Do you really think He will withhold His hand of blessing if you devote yourselves to care for those in need—the people who are most on His heart? No way! God isn't watching and saying, "You know, I think I'll let that church fall apart because they're selflessly serving the vulnerable people in their community." Never. Not going to happen. Again and again, I've seen God provide for ministries of compassion. I have no doubt He'll provide for every church that gets involved.

Third, as your church develops a reputation as a caring body of believers, people will be attracted to it. Some will be the poor people who need more help, but also those with means will want to be a part of something that's changing lives, and they'll give. Let me assure you, Love Where You Live more than pays for itself. It's not a slick marketing tactic that guarantees a return on investment; it's the way the kingdom of God operates.

Love Where You Live *surfaces* needs but *focuses* on solutions. That matters because people are far more motivated to give when they're convinced they'll get to participate in bringing effective, tangible solutions to the community's nagging needs.

> People are far more motivated to give when they're convinced they'll get to participate in bringing effective, tangible solutions to the community's nagging needs.

Some of you have read this far and wonder if you can marshal enough people and resources to make a dent in the community. You can. You can start small, do what you do with a wonderful blend of joy and excellence, master the art of telling stories, schedule the next LWYL event and the next, and watch the momentum build. Some of the churches who have been part of Love Where You Live for several years started with two Saturdays a year, then had two Saturdays twice a year, then a month of Saturdays twice a year. And their participation has grown at every stage.

Good Citizens

Jesus turned the values of the world upside down and inside out. The world values power, prestige, and popularity, but Jesus made himself vulnerable, an outcast, and despised. Other religions, including the secular religion of success that's practiced by millions, are based on the premise that the good are rewarded, but the gospel is the polar opposite: Jesus died for sinners, the ungrateful, and those who had nothing that could impress Him—in other words, those who admit they aren't good and need a Savior.

Jesus taught and demonstrated that true success isn't having power over people; it's serving them. When His disciples argued about who would be the greatest when Jesus inaugurated His kingdom, He took off His robe and took the role of the lowest servant to wash their feet. What's distinct about Him? He had it all and gave it all . . . for you and me. What's distinct about those who truly follow Him? We're known by our love for people, especially people in His family and those who can't give back.

Tommy Barnett, pastor of Dream City Church in Phoenix, Arizona, has a crystal-clear ministry philosophy: "Find a need and fill it; find a hurt and heal it." That's the essence of Love Where You Live. My good friend Hal Donaldson, the president and founder of Convoy Hope, has a similar perspective: "Jesus hides Himself among the needy." In other words, if you want to know Jesus, get involved in caring for the poor, widows, orphans, immigrants, single moms, addicts, the elderly, the sick, and the forgotten. Jesus' heart leans toward these people, and when we have even the faintest grasp of His grace, our hearts lean that way too.

Still wondering if it's for you? Love Where You Live is the avenue for church leaders to fulfill virtually every goal for their people.

- Do you want your people to develop a heart like Jesus? Put them in touch with the people Jesus cares for.
- Do you want them to give more generously and gladly? Let their hearts be touched by the crying needs in the

community, and they'll open their wallets and purses more widely.

- Do you want leaders to rise up? Put people in roles that inflame their passions, and watch them serve with excellence.
- Do you want to turn your people away from petty arguments to genuine unity? Let them sweat together, paint together, rake together, and bake cookies together. Encourage unity by enacting it rather than just talking about it—it's an engaging teaching style.
- Do you want your church to grow? Care for people outside the church. Then people will come because they've been personally touched by love, they want to be part of a caring community, and they want to see if this kind of love is real.
- Do you want your church to be seen as the go-to resource in the city and especially among city leaders? Develop a reputation of giving, sharing, and loving people who are often overlooked or seen as a nuisance, and you'll have a reputation as a trustworthy partner of community leaders. Most of the city officials know they can't meet all the needs they face, and they'll be glad to have you and your people on board.

Of course you want all this for your people. You wouldn't have read this far if you didn't. Who wouldn't want to be part of something like this?

Well, then, what are you waiting for?

create a movement

THINK ABOUT IT

1. Have you ever been part of something that could be described as a movement? If so, describe the impact it had on you and others. If not, what do you imagine it would be like?

2. How do the principles of the rock and the flywheel apply to you and your efforts to implement Love Where You Live?

3. What difference would it make if your church created such a powerful movement of love that serving became the norm?

4. In which stage of church growth and development is your church? How does this understanding help you make progress with Love Where You Live?

5. Which of the benefits in the last section of this chapter (the questions and answers listed) are most appealing to you? Explain your answer. What does (or will) it look like when God works in all these ways?

PRAY ABOUT IT

Thank God for His purpose to make Himself known through the love of people in your church, and ask Him for direction and enthusiasm as you take steps to implement Love Where You Live.

DO IT

If you're a pastor or church leader, go to LoveWhere YouLive.church to access a free Love Where You Live bonus packet, which provides resources and ideas to help you successfully launch your LWYL event.

Buy a copy of this book (at a discount on the website) for adults and high school students in the church. You can ask them to pay the church back, or this can be part of the expenses of your Love Where You Live program.

Distribute the books, preach the sermon series, teach the principles in your small groups, and co-ordinate the first (or next) LWYL Saturdays . . . and watch God work.

Begin developing relationships with leaders in the community by serving them with joy and excellence. As you anticipate the upcoming LWYL event, look ahead to schedule your next outreach so you can maintain momentum and get ahead of the planning curve.

If you're a church member, encourage your pastor to launch Love Where You Live. Offer your support, time, and resources to get it going or take it to the next level. No matter the response, find a few people to join you, find an organization to help, and dive in. More people will join you next time.

using *indispensable church* in small groups and classes

This book is designed for individual study, small groups, and classes. The best way to absorb and apply these principles is for each person to individually study and answer the questions at the end of each chapter, then discuss them in either a class or a group environment.

Each chapter's questions are designed to promote reflection, application, and discussion. Order enough copies of the book for each person to have a copy. For couples, encourage both to have their own book so they can record their individual reflections.

Here is a recommended schedule for a small group or class:

Week 1: Introduce the material. As a group leader, tell your story about how someone has loved you and changed your life, or how God has used your love for others to change theirs. Share your hopes for the group. Encourage people to read the assigned chapter(s) each week and answer the questions.

Weeks 2–10: Each week, introduce the topic for the week and share a story of how God has used the principles in your life. In small groups, lead people through a discussion of the questions at the end of the chapter. In classes, teach the principles in each chapter, use personal illustrations, and invite discussion.

Personalize Each Lesson

Don't feel pressured to cover every question in your group discussions. Pick out three or four that had the biggest impact on you and focus on those, or ask people in the group to share their responses to the questions that meant the most to them that week.

Make sure you personalize the principles and applications. At least once in each group meeting, add your own story to illustrate a particular point.

Make the Scriptures come alive. Far too often, we read the Bible like it's a phone book, with little or no emotion. Paint a vivid picture for people. Provide insights about the context of people's encounters with God, and help those in your group or class sense the emotions of specific people in each scene.

Focus on Application

The questions at the end of each chapter and your encouragement to group members to put love into action will help them take big steps to apply the principles they're learning. Share how you are applying the principles each week.

Consider Three Types of Questions

If you have led groups for a few years, you already understand the importance of using open questions to stimulate discussion. Three types of questions are limiting, leading, and open.

Limiting questions focus on an obvious answer, such as, "What does Jesus call himself in John 10:11?" They don't stimulate reflection or discussion. If you want to use questions like these, follow them with thought-provoking, open questions.

Leading questions require the listener to guess what the leader has in mind, such as, "Why did Jesus use the metaphor of a shepherd in John 10?" (He was probably alluding to a passage in Ezekiel, but most people don't know that.) The teacher who asks a leading question has a definite answer in mind. Instead of asking this kind of question, teach the point and ask an open question about that point.

Open questions usually don't have right or wrong answers. They stimulate thinking, and they are far less threatening because the person answering doesn't risk ridicule for being wrong. These questions often begin with "Why do you think . . . ?" or "What are some reasons that . . . ?" or "How would you have felt in that situation?" Many of the questions at the end of each chapter are open ones.

Prepare

As you prepare to teach this material in a group or class, consider these steps:

1. Carefully and thoughtfully read the book. Make notes; highlight key sections, quotes, or stories; and complete

the "Think about It" section at the end of each chapter. This will familiarize you with the entire scope of the content.

2. As you prepare for each week's group or class, read the corresponding chapter again and make additional notes.

3. Tailor the amount of content to the time allotted. You may not have time to cover all the questions, so pick the ones that are most pertinent.

4. Add your own stories to personalize the message and add impact.

5. Before and during your preparation, ask God to give you wisdom, clarity, and power. Trust Him to use your group to change people's lives.

6. Encourage each person to read the chapter and complete the "Think about It" section each week. Most people will get far more out of the group in doing so.

notes

Chapter 2 Love Is a Verb

1. *Talladega Nights: The Ballad of Ricky Bobby*, directed by Adam McKay (Culver City, CA: Columbia Pictures, 2006), DVD.

2. B. B. Warfield, "The Emotional Life of Our Lord," Monergism, accessed August 5, 2020, https://www.monergism.com/thethreshold/articles /onsite/emotionallife.html.

Chapter 3 My Neighbor

1. "Executive Summary," SurgeonGeneral.gov, accessed September 15, 2020, https://addiction.surgeongeneral.gov/executive-summary.

Chapter 4 Why Is It So Hard?

1. Christian Smith with Melinda Lundquist Denton, *Soul Searching* (New York: Oxford University Press, 2005), 125–41.

2. This is the title of an excellent book by Eugene Peterson.

3. Bryan Chapell, "Lecture 1: The Heart of a Christ-Centered Message," Biblical Training, accessed August 6, 2020, https://www.biblicaltraining.org /library/heart-christ-centered-message/introduction-public-speaking /bryan-chapell.

4. Augustine, *Sermons* 191.1.

5. Larry Crabb, *Finding God* (Zondervan: Grand Rapids, 1993), 18.

6. Charles Wesley, "And Can It Be?," Sovereign Grace Music, 1738.

7. Rodney Stark, *The Rise of Christianity* (New York: HarperCollins, 1966), 7.

8. Thucydides, *History of the Peloponnesian War*, 2:47–55.
9. Dionysius, quoted in Stark, *Rise of Christianity*, 83.
10. Dionysius, quoted in Stark, *Rise of Christianity*, 82.

Chapter 5 The Call

1. Os Guinness, *The Call* (Nashville: Word Publishing, 1998), 4.
2. Guinness, *The Call*, 30.

Chapter 6 Start Small . . . but Start!

1. For much more on how Christians relate to culture, see Richard Niebuhr, *Christ and Culture* (New York: Harper and Row, 1951), or a synopsis of the book's views by Focus on the Family: https://www.focusonthefamily.ca/content/christ-and-culture-five-views.
2. Cornelius Plantinga Jr., "Sin: Not the Way It's Supposed to Be," 2010, https://tgc-documents.s3.amazonaws.com/cci/Pantinga.pdf.
3. "Foster Care," Children's Rights, accessed on September 20, 2019, https://www.childrensrights.org/newsroom/fact-sheets/foster-care.
4. Rebecca Randall, "How Many Churches Does America Have? More Than You Expected," *Christianity Today*, September 14, 2017, https://www.christianitytoday.com/news/2017/september/how-many-churches-in-america-us-nones-nondenominational.html.

Chapter 8 Woven into the Fabric

1. C. S. Lewis, *The Four Loves* (New York: HarperCollins, 1960), 83.

Chapter 9 Create a Movement

1. For more about this, see Bill Bush, "'Ice Bucket Challenge' Charity Fundraiser Gains Momentum," *Columbus Dispatch*, August 16, 2014, https://www.dispatch.com/article/20140816/NEWS/308169896.

about the author

Chris Sonksen is the founder and lead pastor of South Hills Church, a multicampus church with locations nationwide. Over the last several years South Hills has seen tremendous growth and was recognized by *Outreach* magazine in both 2013 and 2014 as one of the top 100 fastest-growing churches in America. Chris also founded Church BOOM, a resource website designed to coach and train pastors worldwide. He has a dynamic speaking style that has given him the opportunity to speak across the nation in both Christian circles and corporate settings for companies such as Verizon and Home Depot.

Chris is the author of *In Search of Higher Ground*, *Handshake*, *When Your Church Feels Stuck: 7 Unavoidable Questions Every Leader Must Answer*, and *Quit Church: Because Your Life Would Be Better If You Did*.

He and his wife, Laura, live in Southern California. They have two adult children, Grace and Aidan.

LEADING A CHURCH IS HARD.
WE MAKE IT EASIER.

Church BOOM's team of successful, seasoned pastors wants to help you face and overcome the obstacles keeping you from experiencing explosive growth in your church.

- Personal Coaching Call Opportunities
- Video Training Modules
- Full Library of Downloadable Resources
- Complete Sermon Series Branding Packages

Learn more about Church BOOM
at **CHURCHBOOM.ORG**.

WE BELIEVE THAT CHURCH
ISN'T JUST A PLACE TO ATTEND
BUT RATHER A COMMUNITY WE
CAN BELONG TO. OUR VISION IS
TO LEAD UNCHURCHED PEOPLE
INTO GROWING RELATIONSHIPS
WITH JESUS CHRIST.

www.SouthHills.org

"A guide to reignite your church's growth."

—ANDY STANLEY, senior pastor at North Point Ministries

When Your Church Feels Stuck poses seven unavoidable questions church leaders must answer before they can chart the unique path to growth for their church. These challenging questions address the key subjects of mission, strategy, values, metrics, team alignment, culture, and services, and the way you and your team answer these questions will help you discover the real reasons your church is stuck—and what steps you need to take in order to facilitate real growth.

 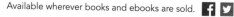

QUIT CHURCH?
Well, not exactly.

Foreword by DAVE FERGUSON

quit
CHURCH

Because Your Life Would Be
Better If You Did

CHRIS SONKSEN

Drawing from his experience coaching hundreds of churches
toward true growth, Chris Sonksen calls on us to quit our
casual, cultural commitment to church as we know it.

BakerBooks
a division of Baker Publishing Group
www.BakerBooks.com

Available wherever books and ebooks are sold.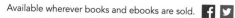

CONNECT WITH CHRIS!

To learn more about his ministry, speaking engagements, and leadership, visit

ChrisSonksen.com

 @ChrisSonksen

 @ChrisSonksen

 @ChrisSonksen
